**MS Wc
for Windows 9**

BOOKS AVAILABLE

By both authors:

BP306 A Concise Introduction to Ami Pro 3
BP327 DOS one step at a time
BP337 A Concise User's Guide to Lotus 1-2-3 for Windows
BP341 MS-DOS explained
BP343 A concise introd'n to Microsoft Works for Windows
·BP346 Programming in Visual Basic for Windows
BP351 WordPerfect 6 explained
BP352 Excel 5 explained
BP353 WordPerfect 6.0 for Windows explained
BP354 Word 6 for Windows explained
BP362 Access one step at a time
BP372 CA-SuperCalc for Windows explained
BP387 Windows one step at a time
BP388 Why not personalise your PC
BP399 Windows 95 one step at a time*
BP400 Windows 95 explained*
BP402 MS Office one step at a time
BP405 MS Works for Windows 95 explained
BP406 MS Word 95 explained
BP407 Excel 95 explained
BP408 Access 95 one step at a time
BP409 MS Office 95 one step at a time
BP415 Using Netscape on the Internet
BP419 Using Microsoft Explorer on the Internet
BP420 E-mail on the Internet
BP426 MS-Office 97 explained
BP428 MS-Word 97 explained
BP429 MS-Excel 97 explained
BP430 MS-Access 97 one step at a time

By Noel Kantaris:

BP232 A Concise Introduction to MS-DOS
BP258 Learning to Program in C
BP259 A Concise Introduction to UNIX*
BP261 A Concise Introduction to Lotus 1-2-3
BP264 A Concise Advanced User's Guide to MS-DOS
BP274 A Concise Introduction to SuperCalc 5
BP284 Programming in QuickBASIC
BP325 A Concise User's Guide to Windows 3.1

MS Works
for Windows 95
explained

by
P.R.M. Oliver
and
N. Kantaris

BERNARD BABANI (publishing) LTD.
THE GRAMPIANS
SHEPHERDS BUSH ROAD
LONDON W6 7NF
ENGLAND

PLEASE NOTE

Although every care has been taken with the production of this book to ensure that any projects, designs, modifications and/or programs, etc., contained herewith, operate in a correct and safe manner and also that any components specified are normally available in Great Britain, the Publishers and Author(s) do not accept responsibility in any way for the failure (including fault in design) of any project, design, modification or program to work correctly or to cause damage to any equipment that it may be connected to or used in conjunction with, or in respect of any other damage or injury that may be so caused, nor do the Publishers accept responsibility in any way for the failure to obtain specified components.

Notice is also given that if equipment that is still under warranty is modified in any way or used or connected with home-built equipment then that warranty may be void.

First Published – April 1996
Reprinted – July 1997
Reprinted – April 1998

British Library Cataloguing in Publication Data:
A catalogue record for this book is available from the British Library

ISBN 0 85934 405 3

Cover Design by Gregor Arthur

Cover illustration by Adam Willis

Printed and bound in Great Britain by Cox & Wyman Ltd, Reading

ABOUT THIS BOOK

This book *MS Works for Windows 95 explained* was written to help the beginner, or those transferring from another version of Microsoft Works. The material in the book is presented on the 'what you need to know first, appears first' basis, but you don't have to start at the beginning and go right through to the end. The more experienced user can start from any section, as they have been designed to be self contained. The book does not, however, describe the workings of Microsoft Windows 95, or how to set up your computer hardware. If you need to know more about these, then may we suggest that you refer to the book *Windows 95 explained* (BP400), which is also published by BERNARD BABANI (publishing) Ltd.

Microsoft Works for Windows 95 (version 4) is a powerful integrated package containing four major types of applications; word processing with drawing, spreadsheet with graphing, database management with reporting, and communications. The last of these applications, communications, is not really covered in this book.

The program has been upgraded to take advantage of the 32-bit features of Windows 95, and includes full support for multi-tasking, OLE 2 and long filenames. The power and versatility of Works for Windows 95 is evident in its integration which allows data from any module to be quickly and easily transferred into any of the other modules. The package is a powerful one, offering many commands, and functions. We found the word processor to be almost as powerful as many of the 'stand alone' packages available today. The missing features are the least used anyway.

Microsoft have gone to town with this version of Works regarding the number and quality of Wizards supplied with the program. We have not, however, spent much time describing them for two good reasons:

1. They are very user friendly and almost anyone should be able to work through them without too many problems.

2. We feel strongly that you will become more proficient with the Works for Windows program, as a whole, if you build your own applications.

If you want to start off using these 'tailor made' files and documents, have a look through Chapter 9, before getting too much further in the book.

This book is intended as a supplement to the on-line Help material, and to the very limited documentation that now seems to come with Microsoft's packages. It will provide the new user with a set of examples that will help with the learning of the most commonly used features of the package, and also help provide the confidence needed to tackle some of the more advanced features later.

Companion Discs

If you would like to purchase a floppy disc containing all the files/programs which appear in this, or any other book(s) by the same author(s), (except for those marked with an asterisk on the list at the front of this book), then fill in the form at the back and send it to P. R. M. Oliver at the address stipulated.

ABOUT THE AUTHORS

Phil Oliver graduated in Mining Engineering at Camborne School of Mines in 1967 and since then has specialised in most aspects of surface mining technology, with a particular emphasis on computer related techniques. He has worked in Guyana, Canada, several Middle Eastern countries, South Africa and the United Kingdom, on such diverse projects as: the planning and management of bauxite, iron, gold and coal mines; rock excavation contracting in the UK; international mining equipment sales and technical back up and international mine consulting for a major mining house in South Africa. In 1988 he took up a lecturing position at Camborne School of Mines (part of Exeter University) in Surface Mining and Management.

Noel Kantaris graduated in Electrical Engineering at Bristol University and after spending three years in the Electronics Industry in London, took up a Tutorship in Physics at the University of Queensland. Research interests in Ionospheric Physics, led to the degrees of M.E. in Electronics and Ph.D. in Physics. On return to the UK, he took up a Post-Doctoral Research Fellowship in Radio Physics at the University of Leicester, and then in 1973 a lecturing position in Engineering at the Camborne School of Mines, Cornwall, (part of Exeter University), where since 1978 he has also assumed the responsibility for the Computing Department.

TRADEMARKS

ACKNOWLEDGEMENTS

We would like to thank the staff of Text 100 Limited for providing the software programs on which this work was based. We would also like to thank colleagues at the Camborne School of Mines for the helpful tips and suggestions which assisted us in the writing of this book.

CONTENTS

1. PACKAGE OVERVIEW

Microsoft Works for Windows 95 is an easy to use, integrated package, which incorporates four main modules; word processing, spreadsheet with chart graphics, database, and communications, all of which are downward compatible with earlier Windows and DOS versions. Microsoft Draw is included, which allows you to create or modify pictures in the word processor. Only if you have a modem will the communications features be of interest to you. The package, as its name would suggest, operates inside the graphic interface provided by Microsoft Windows 95. It comes with some documentation and with WorksWizards. Do not let the name WorksWizards put you off, they simplify many common procedures by stepping you through semi-automated routines.

Installing Works

Microsoft Works for Windows 95 can be installed on an IBM compatible PC that has a working copy of Microsoft Windows 95 already installed. It needs about 14MB of hard disc space for a full installation. If necessary you could reduce this considerably, in the future, by dispensing with the tutorial and example files. The procedure takes about half an hour and is very easy, involving transferring the working files from a CD-ROM, or 3.5 inch floppy system discs, to your hard disc and uncompressing them.

To carry out the installation, start Windows 95 in the usual way and insert the Works Setup disc (No. 1) in your A: drive, or the CD-ROM in its drive. Click **Start** on the Taskbar, then **Run** from the opened menu and type

    A:Setup

in the **Open** box that appears. Where 'A' is the letter of the floppy or CD-ROM drive holding the new Works disc. Pressing the <Enter> key will produce an opening Setup screen. Our version of Works came with Bookshelf '95 included, as shown on the next page. Yours may be different, but the basic procedures should be very similar.

1

Clicking the **Install Microsoft Works 4.0** button will open the Welcome screen shown below.

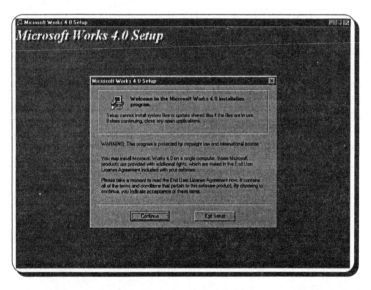

If necessary, close any open applications as requested. The easiest way to do this is from the menu that opens when their Taskbar icon is right-clicked with the mouse.

You will then be be asked for details of your name and company and for the CD key number of your version of

Works. Hopefully you will find this on a sticker on the outside of the CD-ROM box.

Select **OK** to accept each screen and either accept C:\Program Files\MSWorks as the location folder for the installation, or use the **Change Folder** option. You then get the choice of a **Complete**, or a **Custom** installation. We will assume you use the **Complete Installation** but if there is not enough space on your hard disc drive, you should use the other option.

Accept the Shortcut offer by pressing **Yes** and the file copying procedure will start with the bottom window frame keeping you informed about what is happening. If required, you will be asked to place the next disc into the A: drive. At least the series of information and advertising screens help to relieve the boredom!

When the fairly painless operation is complete you should see the window shown here. If you are connected to the outer World, you can click the **Online Registration** button to send your details to Microsoft. But what information will they be given about your set-up? Big brother is getting nearer and nearer! Selecting **OK** will complete the installation.

Hopefully you should have a successful installation and when you return to the Windows desktop there should be a new Shortcut icon, as shown on the next page. Also, when you open the cascading **Start** menus there should be several Works options, similar to those shown. What actually displays will depend on your version of Works.

The **Microsoft Works 4.0 Setup** option is used to reactivate the Setup program if you need to make any changes in the future. **Introduction to Microsoft Works 4.0** opens a tour of the package. This is offered to you automatically the first time you run Works, perhaps that would be a good time to 'take the tour'.

3

Starting Works

There are two ways to start the Works program for the first time, by double clicking the Shortcut to Microsoft Works 4.0 icon shown above, or to select Microsoft Works 4.0 from the opened cascade menu. When the program is opened the following Task Launcher dialogue box is displayed.

This has three tabbed sections, the default one giving rapid access to all the **TaskWizards** that come with the package. If you want to use these, fine, but we will spend some time getting used to the different tools that make up the Works program. For a brief description of the **TaskWizards** you could look at Chapter 9, otherwise click

the **Works Tools** tab to change the Launcher to that shown here.

The **Word Processor** button has a dotted square box (the focus) around its icon, indicating that this is the default option, which will be activated if the <Enter> key is pressed. Pressing the <Tab> key will move this 'default marker' from button to button. It is much easier, though, to click on it with the mouse. These buttons allow you to open a new file in one of Work's four tools.

The **Existing Documents** tab option is used to open files already created in Works. A list of previous files (if any!) is displayed and double-clicking on one of them will rapidly open it in the relevant Works tool.

We suggest you experiment with these options later, but at the moment simply press the <Esc> key, or select **Cancel**, to obtain the basic, or common, Works menu screen, shown below.

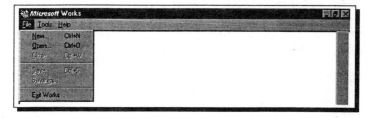

The main Works menu, as shown here, has the item 'File' in the menu highlighted, with its pull-down sub-menu displayed underneath. The pull-down sub-menus associated with the other two items of the main menu can be seen by pressing the right arrow key. Pressing the <Esc> key clears the sub-menus.

The Main Menu:

To activate the main menu, either use the mouse to point to an item; or press the <Alt> key, which causes the first item of the menu (in this case **File**) to be highlighted, then use the right and left arrow keys to highlight any of the items in the main menu. Pressing either the <Enter> key, or the left mouse button, reveals the pull-down sub-menu of the highlighted menu item.

Main menu options can also be activated directly by pressing the <Alt> key followed by the underlined letter of the required option. Thus pressing <Alt+o>, causes the one item pull-down sub-menu of **Tools** to be displayed. You can use the up and down arrow keys to move the highlighted bar up and down a sub-menu, or the right and left arrow keys to move along the options of the main menu. As each option is highlighted, a short description of the function of the relevant option or command appears in the status line at the bottom of the screen. Pressing the <Enter> key selects the highlighted option, or executes the highlighted command. Pressing the <Esc> key closes the menu system and returns you to the main menu.

Selection of a sub-menu item can also be achieved by either typing the underlined letter of the required command, or using the mouse to point to the required command and pressing the left mouse button.

If you use a mouse, there is a quick way of selecting an item from the main menu by pointing to it and pressing the left mouse button; then, with the button depressed, drag the mouse down the revealed sub-menu which highlights each sub-menu item in turn. Once the required item has been highlighted, release the mouse button to select it.

The Main Menu Options:

Each item of the main menu offers the following options:

File   Produces a pull-down menu, as shown, of mainly file related tasks, such as creating a new file, opening an existing file from disc

6

and displaying it on screen, saving and closing a file and exiting Works.

Tools   This menu lets you access, or create, an address book, or change the default settings for Works.

Help   Gives a package overview, offers advice on how to use help, controls a help window on the right of your screen, launches a network forum if you are connected and shows information on your Works set-up.

Note that some sub-menu options, such as the **Save** option of the **File** menu, appear in fainter grey text than, say, the **Open** option. This means that you cannot access them. In this particular instance you cannot save work you have not yet created.

Works Help System

The new Works Help system has been completely re-written. By default now, as shown below, you get a help window

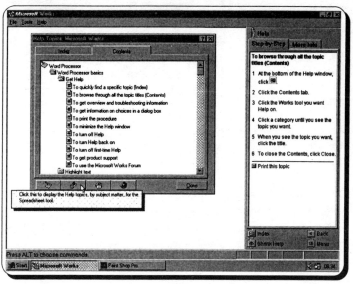

'permanently' open on the right side of the screen. The contents of this window will depend on the Works tool you are using. You control what is displayed in the Help window in two ways:

- By clicking the 'hand' pointer on options in the window opening menu screen.

- By clicking the **Index** button (at the bottom of the window) to open the Help Topics box shown on the previous page, and searching the **Index** or **Contents** lists to find what you want.

The **Contents** list is hierarchical to make it easy to find your way round. In fact a set of instructions for doing this is

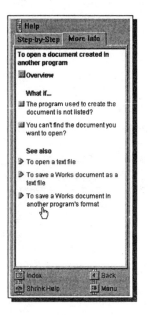

included in our previous example. If you right click your mouse on a feature in the dialogue box a short explanation of its function will 'pop up'.

Whatever subject you choose the Help window gives **Step-by-Step** instructions on how to carry out the operation. To get extra details, click the **More Info** tab and work through its menu options. Remember that when the mouse pointer turns to a hand, as shown here on the left, you can click on the item below to open another page of help information.

Clicking the **Back** button steps you back through your previous choices, one page at a time. The **Menu** button opens the initial Help menu for the tool being used.

You should spend some time exploring the Help system; it is quite detailed, which is just as well as it is the only real source of information about Works that is provided. Most things are in there, you just have to find them!

Dialogue Boxes:

Three periods after a sub-menu option or command, means that a dialogue box will open when the option is selected. A dialogue box lets you enter additional information, such as the name of a file, or lets you change settings.

To illustrate how they work, select the **Tools**, **Options**, command which will display the tabbed dialogue box shown below.

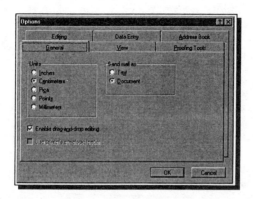

You usually move round a dialogue box with the mouse, but the <Tab> key can be used to move the highlight from one field to the next, (<Shift+Tab> moves the cursor backwards) or alternatively you can move directly to a desired field by holding the <Alt> key down and pressing the underlined letter in the field name. Within a group of options you can use the arrow keys to move from one option to another. Having selected an option or typed in information, you must press a command button such as the **OK** or **Cancel** button, or choose from additional options. To select the **OK** button with the mouse, simply point and click, while with the keyboard, you must first press the <Tab> key until the dotted rectangle, called the focus, moves to the required button, and then press the <Enter> key.

Some dialogue boxes, as on the **Proofing Tools** tab, contain combi boxes which show a column of available choices when their right arrow is clicked. If there are more choices than can be seen

9

in the area provided you use the scroll bars to reveal them. To select a single item from a List box, either double-click the item, or use the arrow keys to highlight the item and press <Enter>.

 Dialogue boxes may contain Option, or radio, buttons with a list of mutually exclusive items, as in the **General** tab. The default choice is marked with a black dot against its name.

 Another type of dialogue box option is the Check box, which can be seen on the **View** tab, this offers a list of features you can switch on or off. Selected options show a tick in the box against the option.

If you can't work out the function of something in a dialogue box there are two quick ways of getting context sensitive help. Clicking the **?** button, next to the Close button in the top right corner of the box, will add a question mark to the pointer. Click this on the unknown item and an explanation window will open up. Alternatively, right clicking the mouse directly on an option will open the same text window.

To cancel a dialogue box, either press the **Cancel** button, or press the <Esc> key enough times, to close the dialogue box and then the menu system.

The Works Screen:

It is perhaps worth spending some time looking at the various parts that make up the Works 95 screen. To illustrate our discussion, click the **Works Tools** tab in the Launcher box and select **Spreadsheet** by pressing 'S', or by clicking its button with your mouse. Note that the screen window produced now displays a new list of menu names at the top, a Toolbar with a series of pictorial icons below, a window title (Unsaved Spreadsheet 1, in this case) below this, an empty worksheet with numbered rows and lettered columns, and the Help window reduced to a thin strip down the right side of the screen with two control buttons.

Works follows the usual Microsoft Windows 95 conventions and if you are familiar with these you can skip through this section. Otherwise a few minutes might be well spent here.

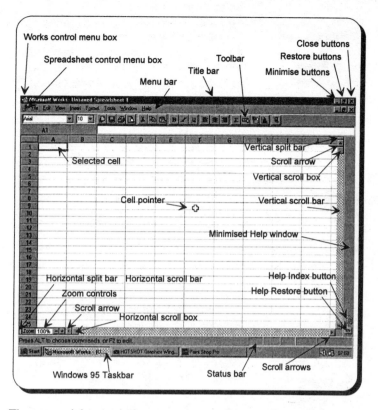

Works control menu box

Spreadsheet control menu box

Menu bar

Title bar

Toolbar

Close buttons
Restore buttons
Minimise buttons

Vertical split bar

Selected cell

Scroll arrow

Vertical scroll box

Cell pointer

Vertical scroll bar

Minimised Help window

Horizontal split bar   Horizontal scroll bar

Help Index button

Zoom controls

Help Restore button

Scroll arrow

Horizontal scroll box

Windows 95 Taskbar

Status bar

Scroll arrows

The spreadsheet window, as shown above, takes up the full screen area available. If you click on the document restore button, the lower one of the two restore buttons at the top right of the screen, you can make it show in a smaller window. This can be useful when you are working with several sheets, or documents, at the same time and you want to transfer between them with the mouse. Although multiple worksheet, database and document files can be displayed simultaneously in their own windows, you can only enter data into the active window (highlighted at the top). Title bars of non active windows appear a lighter shade than that of the active one.

The Works 95 screen is divided into several areas which have the following functions. These are described from the top of the screen down, working from left to right.

Area	*Function*
Control boxes	Clicking on the top control menu box, which is located in the upper left corner of the window, displays the pull-down Control menu which can be used to control the program window. It includes commands for re-sizing, moving, maximising, minimising and closing the window. The lower menu box controls the current document window in the same manner.
Title bar	The bar at the top of a window which displays the application name and the name of the current document.
Minimise buttons	Clicking the top of these reduces Works to an icon on the Taskbar. You click this icon to restore the Works window and even maintain the cursor position. The lower minimise button reduces the document to an icon at the bottom of the Works window.
Restore buttons	When clicked on, these buttons restore the active window to the position and size occupied before being maximised or minimised. The restore button is then replaced by a Maximise button, which is used to set the window to its former size.
Close buttons	The Windows 95 new X buttons that you click to close an application, or document window.
Menu bar	The bar below the title bar which allows you to choose from several menu options. The names of the main menu commands might be different when using different Works tools.

Toolbar	Displays a set of icons for each tool, which can be clicked to quickly carry out menu commands or functions.
Scroll bars	The areas on the screen (right and bottom of each window) that contain scroll boxes in vertical and horizontal bars. Clicking on these bars allows you to control the part of a document which is visible on the screen.
Scroll arrows	The arrowheads at each end of each scroll bar which you can click to scroll the screen up and down one line, or left and right one cell, at a time.
Help 'window'	The minimised window that you can open (by clicking the Help Restore button) to display help text alongside your document.
Status bar	The bottom line of the window that displays the current program status and information regarding the present process.

Manipulating Windows

Works allows the display of multiple sets of data within a given application tool, or several windows encompassing files from different tools, each within its own window.

You will need to manipulate these windows, by selecting which is the active one, moving them so that you can see all the relevant parts of an application, re-sizing them, or indeed closing unwanted windows once you have finished with them. A short discussion follows on how to manipulate windows so that you can get the best of what Works 95 can provide.

In order to illustrate our discussion, use the **File, New** menu command three successive times and open some more spreadsheet and word processor documents. As each selection is made, a new, titled, window is displayed, with new windows being placed on top of any existing ones.

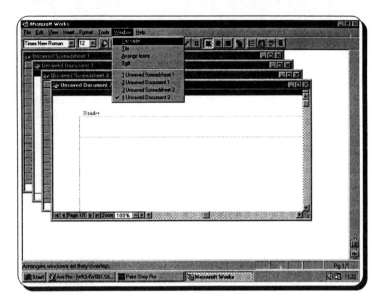

If you create a certain type of window file using the same tool more than once in any work session, this is reflected in the number appearing immediately after the default name of that particular window. You should save your work using different names from these default ones. Note that the active window has a highlighted title bar, while the non active title bars are dimmed.

The **Window** menu option is used to control the display of your opened windows. As shown in our example above, they are in **Cascade** form.

Changing the Active Window:

You can select the active window, from amongst those displayed on the screen, by pointing to any part of it, and clicking the left mouse button, or by selecting the **Window** command of the main menu and choosing the appropriate number of the window you want to make the active one.

14

Closing a Window:

Works itself, or any tool window (provided it is the active window), can be closed at any time, maybe to save screen space and memory. There are several ways to close the active window; the easiest is to click on its Close button (the X button in the top right hand corner), also you can double click on the File Control Menu Box (the icon in the upper-left corner of the window), or press the <Ctrl+F4> keys, or use the **File, Close** command.

If you have made any changes to a file in a window since the last time you saved it, Works will warn you with the appearance of a dialogue box giving you the option to save the file before closing it.

Moving Windows and Dialogue Boxes:

When you have multiple windows or dialogue boxes on the screen, you might want to move a particular one to a different part of the screen. This can be achieved with either the mouse or the keyboard, but not if the window occupies the full screen, for obvious reasons.

To move a window, or a dialogue box, with the mouse, point to the title bar and drag it (press the left button and keep it pressed while moving the mouse) until the shadow border is where you want it to be. Then release the mouse button to fix it into its new position.

To move with the keyboard, press <Alt+Spacebar> to reveal the Application Control Menu, or <Alt+−> to reveal the Document Control menu. Then, press 'M', to select **Move,** which causes a four-headed arrow to appear in the title bar and use the arrow keys to move the shadow border of the window to the required place. Press <Enter> to fix the window to its new position, or <Esc> to cancel the relocation.

Sizing a Window:

You can change the size of a window with either the mouse or the keyboard. To size an active window with the mouse, move the window so that the side you want to change is visible, then move the mouse pointer to the edge of the window or corner, so that it changes to a two-headed arrow, then drag the two-headed arrow in the direction you want that

15

side or corner to move. Continue dragging until the shadow border is the size you require, then release the mouse button.

To size with the keyboard, press either <Alt+Spacebar> or <Alt+–> to reveal the Application Control menu or the Document Control menu, then press 'S' to select **Size**, which causes the four-headed arrow to appear. Now press the arrow key that corresponds to the edge you want to move, or if a corner, press the two arrow keys (one after the other) corresponding to the particular corner, which causes the pointer to change to a two-headed arrow. Press an appropriate arrow key in the direction you want that side or corner to move and continue to do so until the shadow border is the size you require, then press <Enter> to fix the new window size.

Splitting a Window:

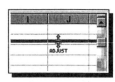

The windows of two Works application tools can be split, so that you can see different parts of your work side by side in the same window. You can split the word processor window horizontally and the spreadsheet window both horizontally and vertically.

To split a window, move the mouse pointer onto a split bar (the bar either above the top scroll arrow, or to the left of the zoom controls), drag the new pointer shape to the required

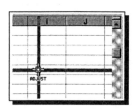

position (as shown in our example above), and release the mouse button. Otherwise you could use the **Window, Split** command, then the arrow keys to move the shadow split lines, as shown alongside, to the required position and press <Enter>. To cancel the operation press <Esc>.

The figure on the next page shows the word processor window active and split into two areas and the spreadsheet window split into four areas.

16

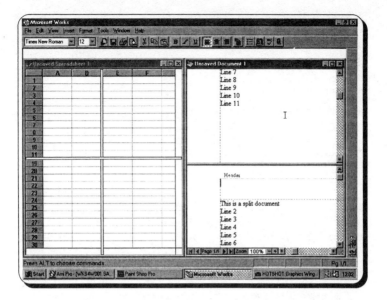

Viewing All Windows:

You can arrange to view all the windows currently on the screen by using the **Window**, **Tile** command. Works automatically arranges the windows on screen. Three windows are placed full screen height and next to each other, while four will occupy a quarter of the screen each. If you are experimenting with the program as you go, watch how the mouse pointer changes shape, depending on where it is and what it is doing.

Managing Files

With Works you can create, save, open, or generally operate on files, by using the **File** command from the menu bar, or by using toolbar icons.

Saving a File:

Once a document has been prepared, under any of the tool applications, you can save it by using the **File, Save**

 command, or by clicking the Save toolbar icon. The first time you use this command with, say, the word processor, Works opens the Save As

dialogue box, shown here. You type a new name without any extension (see bottom of next page) in the **File name** text box. A new 'Documents' folder should have been opened automatically when Works was installed, so unless you want to store your work somewhere else just accept this destination in the **Save in** text box. Pressing **Save**, or the <Enter> key, causes your typed filename to become the new document title. Once a file has been saved, subsequent use of the **File, Save** command, saves the file automatically under that filename, and in the same folder as you first saved your work.

If you want to save an already saved file under a different name, then use the **File, Save As** command. Works for Windows 95 again offers you, in the same dialogue box, the original filename which you can change by typing a different name, without an extension (the moment you start typing the new name, the default name vanishes from the display). On pressing <Enter>, the program adds automatically the appropriate extension for you and saves the file.

The **Save as type** list box allows you to save the file in any of the formats listed. For example, you would select 'WordPerfect 5.1 for MS-DOS', if you wanted to use the file later in that package. As usual Microsoft's list of supported file conversion filters is anything but complete, and nowhere near up to date.

Retrieving a File:
To retrieve an already saved document from disc, use the **File, Open** menu command from whatever tool window you are in. This will bring up the standard Windows 95 Open dialogue box, as shown on the facing page.

18

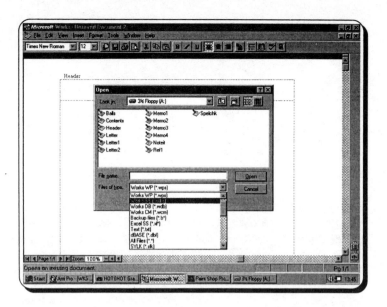

In this case the open folder is our A: disc drive and 'Works
WP (*.wps)' has been selected in the **Files of type** box, so all
the Works word processor files on the disc are shown. To
select a file, you would either click at its name with the mouse
pointer, or press <Alt+n> to move into the **File name** box,
press <Tab> enough times to move the highlight down into
the file list, highlight the required file with the arrow keys and
press <Enter>. The mouse method is definitely preferable!

With Windows 95 you do not need to get involved with file
name extensions, and by default, as shown above, they do
not display. They are used by Windows to determine what
application (or Works tool) is needed to work with the file. But
all the Windows file manipulation dialogue boxes display
icons for the different file types.

  To help you determine which type of file is used with the
Works for Windows 95 tools the filename extensions of the
four application tools are shown with their icons on the next
page.

19

Extension	Icon	Tool
WPS		Works Word Processor
WKS		Works Spreadsheet
WDB		Works Database
WCM		Works Communications

Exiting Works

Whenever you are ready to leave the Works for Windows 95 package the procedure is the same whichever tool you are in. You either use the **File**, **Exit Works** command, or click the application's X Close button, at the top right of the window.

If all the open files have been saved, Works will terminate. If not you will be given the option to save them, before they are 'lost forever'.

One thing to remember, is to close Works before you attempt to close Windows 95. If you don't, you may get the annoying message box shown here, and it takes much longer to get your PC turned off.

20

2. THE WORKS WORD PROCESSOR

Works for Windows 95 comes equipped with a word processor almost as powerful as most 'stand alone' versions. It has all the normal editing features, including the ability to insert, delete, erase, search for, replace, drag and drop copy and move characters, lines and whole blocks of text. As you would expect, it also allows you to enhance text and create bold, underlined, italic, strike-through, superscript, subscript and other specially formatted text. Being an integrated package it is easy to embed part of a spreadsheet into a document, carry out a mail merge, or send a document to a distant computer using the communications functions.

Word Processor Basics

To access the word processor, select the **Works Tools** section of the Task Launcher, as described in the previous chapter. Then select the **Word Processor** button by either pressing the **W** key, or pressing <Enter>, as this is the highlighted option. A screen similar to that shown below will appear. We have opened the Help window, added a ruler and set the screen zoom to 75%.

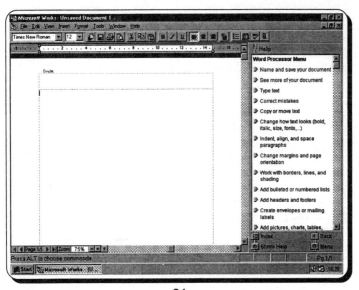

The Word Processor Screen:

The top line of this screen, which has the document window expanded to full size, shows the document title. The next down is the menu bar, which with the word processor, accesses the following sub menus:

<u>F</u>ile <u>E</u>dit <u>V</u>iew <u>I</u>nsert F<u>o</u>rmat <u>T</u>ools <u>W</u>indow <u>H</u>elp

As described in the 'Package Overview' these are accessed either with your mouse, or by pressing the <Alt> key followed by the underlined letter.

The Toolbar occupies the third line down. If you use a mouse you will find this a big time saver, once you get in the habit of using it. If you prefer, you can turn it off by activating the **View**, **Toolbar** command. This is a toggle, when the '√' shows the Toolbar will display, otherwise it will not. The only advantage to be gained by not showing it is you gain one screen line. When you move the mouse pointer over one of the icons a yellow message box showing its function opens up.

To use the Toolbar you simply click the mouse on one of the options, and the command selected will affect all text in the document that is highlighted.

The meanings of all the Toolbar options are explained in more detail below.

Option	*Result*
	Choose a font from available list. Clicking the down arrow (↓) will open the list of fonts.
	Choose from available point sizes. Clicking the arrow (↓) will open the list of sizes

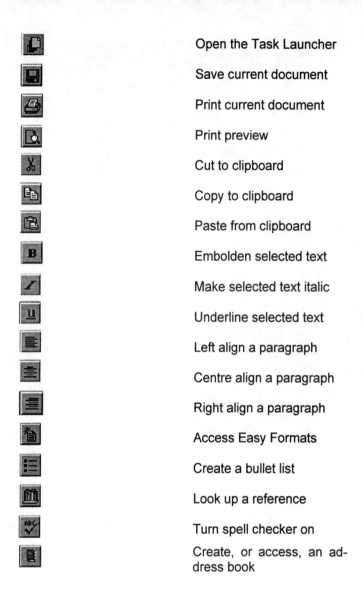

Open the Task Launcher

Save current document

Print current document

Print preview

Cut to clipboard

Copy to clipboard

Paste from clipboard

Embolden selected text

Make selected text italic

Underline selected text

Left align a paragraph

Centre align a paragraph

Right align a paragraph

Access Easy Formats

Create a bullet list

Look up a reference

Turn spell checker on

Create, or access, an address book

This version of Works allows you to change the icons on the toolbar from the Customize Works Toolbar box, opened with the **Tools**, **Customize Toolbar** command.

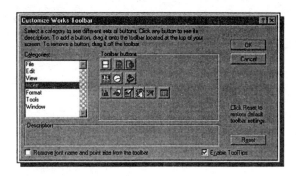

You simply drag any icons you don't want from the toolbar and drag new ones you do from the Toolbar buttons section, as shown above, onto the bar. Press the **Reset** button to abandon your changes.

Below the Toolbar is the ruler which appears as a scale across the screen that can be toggled on and off like the Toolbar, with the **View**, **Ruler** command. This shows and allows you to change the left and right margin positions and any tab or indent settings active in the paragraph the cursor is in. You change the settings by dragging the markers across the ruler.

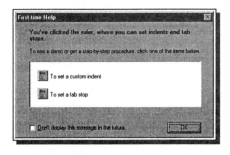

The first time you click the ruler with your mouse pointer a **First-time Help** box like the one shown here appears. This is a new feature of this version of Works, which points you to the relevant Help pages for the 'new' task you are starting on. Make sure you click in the **Dont display this message in the future** box before you click on **OK** to close it.

You can control whether these First-time message boxes appear in the future, by de-selecting **Show first-time Help** in the **View** section of the dialogue box opened with the **Tools**, **Options** menu command. It is worth studying the various options available to you in this box, as shown next.

24

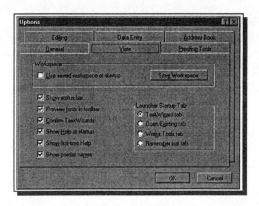

The bottom of the word processing window has a status bar which gives you useful information on the operation being carried out, or a description of the highlighted command, and shows the status of any keys that are currently locked.

The horizontal scroll bar, above the status bar, has a page control feature built into it, as shown here. This lets you change the document page and the zoom factor displayed on the screen. Mouse clicking on the arrow buttons moves the insertion point as shown; and on the + and – buttons

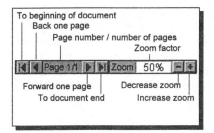

increases and decreases the displayed size of text. A zoom factor of 100% means that screen text is the same size as it will print on paper. The minimum of 50% is half, and the maximum of 400% is four times the printed size.

The other scroll bars, boxes and arrows described in the last chapter also surround the work area which makes up the remainder of the screen.

The working area takes up most of the window. This shows the layout of your page with a series of fine dotted boxes. There is a box for the main text entry area, with a header area outlined above and a footer area below.

25

Entering Text:

Before going any further, click the mouse in the main text entry area and type the memo text shown below, or something else, to get the feel of Works word processing.

```
Header
```

MEMO TO PC USERS
The microcomputers in the Data Processing room are a mixture of IBM compatible PCs with either 486 or Pentium processors. They all have 3.5" floppy drives (of 1.44MB capacity), some also have CD-ROM drives, and others have 5.25" high density drives (of 1.2MB capacity). The PCs are connected to various printers, the Laser printers available give the best results, but are more expensive to use.

The computer you are using will have at least a 512MB hard disc on which a number of software programs, including a version of Windows, have been installed. To make life easier, the hard disc is highly structured with each program installed in a separate directory. When first switched on, the following prompt is displayed:

C:\>

When a new file is opened it is ready for you to begin typing in text. Any time you want to force a new line, or paragraph, just press <Enter>, otherwise the program will sort out line lengths automatically which is known as word wrap. So, you can just carry on typing a complete paragraph without having to press any keys to move to a new line. If you make a mistake, at this stage, press <BkSp> enough times to erase the mistake and retype it.

   Now would be a good time to save the document, as described in the previous chapter, press **File, Save As** and type the filename **Memo1** to save in the Documents folder. Obviously you can change the destination if you want. The program will add the WPS extension for you.

Moving Around a Document:

You can move the cursor around a document by clicking the scroll bars and boxes, with the normal direction keys, with the key combinations shown on the facing page, or with the **Edit**, **Go To** command (or press **F5**). With the last command you can jump to various named 'bookmarks', or to different page numbers, as described later on.

To move	Press
Left one character	←
Right one character	→
Up one line	↑
Down one line	↓
Left one word	Ctrl+←
Right one word	Ctrl+→
Up one paragraph	Ctrl+↑
Down one paragraph	Ctrl+↓
To beginning of line	Home
To end of line	End
To beginning of file	Ctrl+Home
To end of file	Ctrl+End
Up one window	Pg Up
Down one window	Pg Dn

Document Editing

It will not be long when using the word processor before you will need to edit your screen document. This could be to delete unwanted words, to correct a mistake or to add extra text to the document. All these operations are very easy to carry out.

For small deletions, such as letters or words, the easiest method is using the <Del> or <BkSp> keys. With the <Del> key, position the cursor on the first letter to delete and press <Del>; the letter is deleted and the following text moves one space to the left.

With the <BkSp> key, position the cursor immediately to the right of the character to be deleted and press <BkSp>; the cursor moves one space to the left pulling the rest of the line with it and overwriting the character to be deleted.

Word processing is usually carried out in the insert mode. Any characters typed will be inserted at the cursor location and the following text will be pushed to the right, and down, to make room. Pressing the <Ins> key will change you to overstrike mode and the letters 'OVR' will appear on the Status Line. In this mode any text you type will over-write existing text.

To insert blank lines in your text, make sure you are in Insert mode, place the cursor at the beginning of the line where the blank is needed and press <Enter>. The cursor line will move down leaving a blank line. To remove the blank line, position the cursor at its left end and press <Del>.

When larger scale editing is needed, such as using the copy, move and erase operations, the text to be altered must be 'selected', or 'highlighted', before the operation can be carried out. These functions are then available when the **Edit** sub-menu is activated, the Toolbar options used, or Drag and Drop is used.

Selecting Text:

The procedure in Works, as in all Windows applications, is that before any operation such as formatting or editing can be carried out on text, it must first be selected. Selected text is highlighted on the screen. This can be carried out in several ways.

Using the menu you can select all the contents of a document, with the **Edit**, **Select All** command.

Using the keyboard, position the cursor on the first character to be selected and either:

a.   Hold down the <Shift> key while using the direction keys to highlight the required text, then release the <Shift> key, or:

b.   Press the **F8** key and use the direction keys to highlight the required text, or:

c.   Press **F8** *twice* to select a *word*
          Press **F8** *three* times to select a *sentence* (text between stops)
          Press **F8** *four* times to select a *paragraph*
          Press **F8** *five* times to select the whole *document*.

With the mouse:

a.   Left click at the beginning of the block and drag the cursor across the block so that whole words of the desired text are highlighted, then release the mouse button.

b.   With the cursor in a word double-click the left mouse button to select that word.

c.   Position the cursor in the left window margin (where it will change to a right sloping arrow) and then either click the left button to select the current *line*, or double-click the left button to select the current *paragraph*, or hold down the <Ctrl> key and click the left mouse button to select the entire *document*.

When using the **F8** key method, 'EXT' is displayed on the status line with the message 'Selects range of text' to indicate that extended highlighting of text is taking place. The selection can be collapsed one level at a time by pressing <Shift+F8>.

Try out all these methods and find which ones you are most comfortable with.

Copying Blocks of Text:

Once text has been selected it can be copied to another location in your present document, to another Works document (as long as it is open), to another Works tool, or to another Windows program.

As with most of the editing and formatting operations there are several ways of doing this. One is by using the **Edit, Copy** command sequence from the menu, moving the cursor to the start of where you want the copied text, and use the **Edit**, **Paste** command. You can also use toolbar icons, or quick key combinations (details of which are included in Appendix B). Press the Copy icon, or <Ctrl+C>, once the text to be copied has been selected, and the Paste icon, or <Ctrl+V>, to 'paste' it in the new location. These methods do not require the menu bar to be activated.

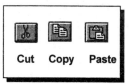

To copy the same text again to another location in the document, move the cursor to the new location and Paste it. This operation is called 'pasting' because of the old days (for some of us) with scissors and a glue pot!

When text is copied, or cut, it is actually placed on the Window's 'clipboard' and remains there until replaced by other text.

Moving Blocks of Text:

Selected text can be moved to any location on the same document. To do this, 'cut' it to the clipboard with the **Edit**, **Cut** command (<Ctrl+X>) and then 'paste' it in the new location with the **Edit**, **Paste** command (<Ctrl+V>). The moved text will be placed at the cursor location and will force any existing text to make room for it. This operation can be cancelled before the final key command by simply pressing <Esc>.

Drag and Drop Editing:

Probably the easiest way to copy and move blocks of text in a document is with the Drag and Drop feature. You have probably noticed that when you move the pointer over a selected block it changes to the DRAG pointer shown.

To move the block, drag it with the left mouse button depressed. To copy it, hold down the <Ctrl> key while you drag.

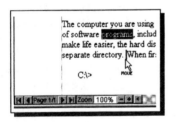

The pointer will change to either a MOVE or COPY arrow and a small vertical bar will follow it around the screen, as shown here. Place this bar at the new start position of the text and release the mouse button. The new text will insert itself where placed, even if the overstrike mode is active. Text moved, or copied, in this way is not placed on the clipboard, so multiple operations are not possible.

Replacing Blocks of Text:

One block of text can be 'replaced' by another using either the cut or copy process. Obviously if cut is used the text at the original location will be removed, but not if the copy command is used. The process is the same as an ordinary copy or move, except that the block of text to be replaced must be selected before the final 'paste' command is made.

Deleting Blocks of Text:

When text is cut or deleted it is removed from the document. With Works for Windows 95 any selected text can be deleted by pressing the <Del> key, or by selecting the **Edit**, **Clear** menu command. This will not, however, place the deleted text on the Windows clipboard, for possible future use. To do this you must use the **Edit**, **Cut** command, icon, or <Ctrl+X>.

The UNDO Command:

As text is lost with the delete command you should use it with caution, but if you do make a mistake all is not lost as long as you act immediately. The **Edit, Undo ..** command reverses your most recent editing or formatting command, so you need to use it before carrying out any further operations. This works even after Drag and Drop actions. Immediately after you undo a command or action, the **Undo ..** command changes to the **Redo ..** command, which allows you to restore what you've reversed. The quick key sequence for the Undo/Redo command is <Ctrl+Z>.

Page Breaks:

The program automatically inserts a page break in a document when a page of typed text is full. There will be places in most multi-page documents where you will want to force a new page to improve the layout. This is done by inserting a manual page break by pressing **Insert**, **Page Break,** or just using the key combination <Ctrl+Enter>. Works readjusts all the non-manual page breaks for the remainder of the document.

A manual page break can be deleted, but an automatic one cannot. Frustratingly, Works for Windows can take several seconds for the screen to sort out its automatic page breaks, especially with a long document, and it can fall behind you. If this becomes a problem simply use the **Tools**, **Paginate Now** command, or **F9**, to force an immediate repagination of the document on screen.

Document Navigation:

There are several methods of navigating large documents in Works. You can use the page control buttons on the horizontal scroll bar, but there are also two methods of jumping to specific document locations. Both use the **Edit**,

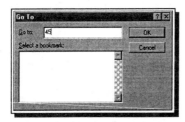

Go To command, or **F5** for short. This brings up the dialogue box shown here.

Typing a page number in the **Go to** text box and pressing **OK**, or <Enter>, should make the cursor jump straight to the top of that page in the document. This is a quick way of moving to the top of any page.

The other method uses the same box but uses 'bookmarks' which you place at strategic locations in your document. To place a bookmark in a document, locate the cursor where you want the mark and select **Edit**, **Bookmark**. Type a name in the empty **Name** text box and then press **OK** to create the invisible bookmark. The next time you press **F5**, your bookmark name should now appear in the box under **Select a bookmark**. Highlight this, press **OK**, and the cursor should jump to where the bookmark was placed. In a long document placing bookmarks at the start of each section makes it easy to find your way around.

Viewing Word Processor Documents

Works provides three ways to view your document on the screen. Each view allows you to concentrate on different aspects of your work. Choose the view you want from the **View** menu, except for **Print Preview** which is on the **File** menu .

Normal View:

This view seems to be 'left over' from previous versions of Works, and shows text and paragraph formatting, line and page breaks, tab and paragraph alignment. Normal view, however, displays only a single column of text and only shows headers and footers on the first page of the document and text does not display as it will print.

Page Layout View:

This fully WYSIWYG (what you see is what you get) view is the default and displays each page in your document as it will look when printed. Columns, headers, footers and footnotes appear in their correct positions and you can edit them in this view. It is also excellent for working with embedded objects, such as pictures and graphics. Page layout view can be slower though if you have a very slow PC.

The Zoom Command:

The Zoom feature, available in the above two views, allows you to control the amount of the active document that will display on the screen at any time. The zoom size status of a particular document has no effect on the document when it is printed. From the **View** menu, choose **Zoom**, and then choose the size you want from the dialogue box as shown here.

With the **Custom** option you can specify any magnification factor between 25 and 1000.

Print Preview:

This shows a view of your document on the screen, one page at a time, exactly as it will be printed. You can't edit text or make any changes in print preview, but you can also zoom the view in and out.

Character Enhancement

Another simplistic example will explain the principles of text enhancement. With Works for Windows 95 it is often easier to type your text in first and worry about the document layout later on. Create a new word processing file and type in the letter text shown (in Normal View) below.

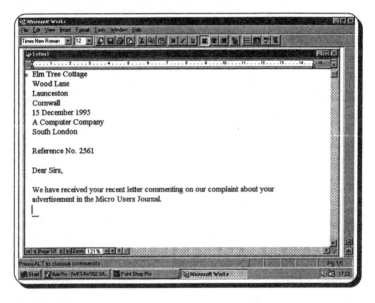

The date on line 5 is not just typed in. A code is embedded so that it will give the current date when the letter is printed. This is generated with the quick key combination <Ctrl+D>, or it can be selected from the dialogue box opened with the **Insert**, **Date and Time** command. When you have finished, save the document using the **File**, **Save As** command, calling it **Letter1**.

34

To improve the layout of the letter we will use some of the commands in the **Format** sub-menu and also some of the Toolbar and Quick key options.

First select the top five lines containing the address and date (the easiest way of doing this is to click the mouse alongside line one, in the left margin, and drag it down to line 5) and then select the **Format**, **Paragraph**, **Indents and Alignment**, command to open the box below. Select the **Alignment** as **Right** as shown below and press **OK**.

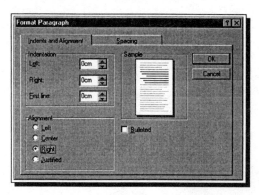

The whole block should now be 'right justified'. By default paragraphs are 'left justified'. While the block is still highlighted press the <Ctrl+L> keys and finally click the mouse on the Right Align icon of the Toolbar. You should now be back with a right justified address.

Then select the Ref... line of text and press **Format**, **Paragraph**, **Indents and Alignment**, **Center** (or the quick keys <Ctrl+E>, or the Centre Align Toolbar icon) to centre the line between the left and right margins. While the selection highlight is still active press **Format**, **Font and Style**, **Underline** (or <Ctrl+U>, or the Underline icon on the Toolbar) to underline the reference. By now you have probably accepted that the Toolbar is by far the most convenient way of carrying out these enhancement functions. If you repeat the Toolbar click, while the highlight is still active, the feature is turned off again; they act as toggle functions.

Next, select the words 'recent letter' and press <Ctrl+B>, or the Bold icon, to embolden them. Finally, select the section

'Micro Users Journal' and change them to italics by pressing **Format, Font and Style, Italic,** or <Ctrl+I>, or the Italic icon.

The letter now looks very different and should be similar to **Letter2**, shown below in Normal View.

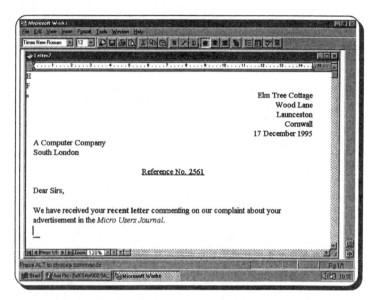

What a difference with only a few keystrokes! Note that when the cursor is in text that has been enhanced, the relevant icon on the Toolbar appears 'depressed'. In the above example the Left Align icon is selected. These status indicators are useful when the enhancements are not obvious from the screen text. Also note that the date has changed. Remember that the date was entered as a code and our two examples were produced on different days.

Fonts:

A font is a typeface with a specific design. In Works for Windows 95 you can work with and print text in any fonts which are supported by your version of Windows 95. You can also work with any supported colours, but only print them if you have a colour printer.

36

To change the font, size, colour or enhancements of specific text in a document, first select the text. Choose the **Font & Style** command either from the **Format** menu, or from the 'object menu' opened by right-clicking the document edit area, and make selections in the opened dialogue box, as shown below.

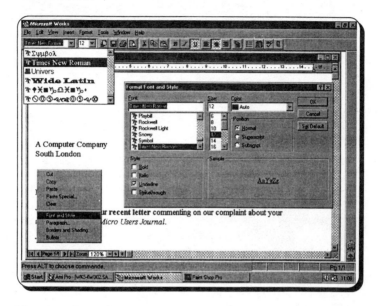

You can also, of course, change the font and size of selected text from the Font Name and Font Size Toolbar icons. Clicking the arrow alongside each opens up a menu of available options.

The composite screen, made up above, shows both methods of changing the font and font size of selected text, as well as the object menu mentioned above. You will not be able to get them all on the screen at the same time, though, so do not bother trying.

The Toolbar icons are by far the best option for carrying out these operations, as is obvious by the way Microsoft have buried the text formatting commands so deeply in the menu system.

Works measures font sizes in points, where one point is 1/72nd of an inch. You will need to study your printer manual and experiment with these commands to make the most of this Works facility.

One thing to remember is that a printed page usually looks better if you use different fonts and sizes sparingly.

3. ADVANCED WP FEATURES

Paragraph Formatting

Works for Windows defines a paragraph, as any text which is followed by a paragraph mark (which appears as a '¶' character on the screen, but only when switched on). So single line titles, as well as long typed text, can form paragraphs. Paragraph markers are not normally shown in Works, but toggling the **View**, **All Characters** command, will toggle them on and off. The example below shows our file **Memo1** with formatting characters switched on. This facility can be very useful when you are laying out a complicated page of data. Note how blank space characters show as a '·' character.

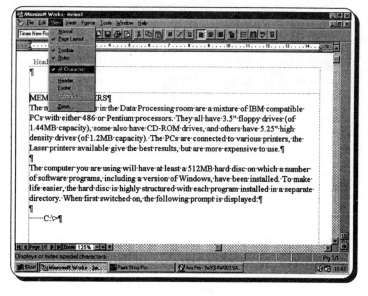

A paragraph marker is placed in a document every time <Enter> is pressed. All paragraph formatting, such as alignment, justification, centring, indenting and line spacing, is stored in the marker for the particular paragraph. If this marker is deleted, or moved, the formatting will be deleted or moved with it.

Indenting Text:

Most documents with lists, or numbered sections, will require some form of paragraph indenting. An indent is the space between the margin and the edge of the text in the paragraph. This can be on the left or right side of the page.

Retrieve the file **Memo1** and type '1. ' and '2. ' before the first words of the two main text paragraphs. Select the two paragraphs and press **Format**, **Paragraph**, **Indents and Alignment** to open the dialogue box below.

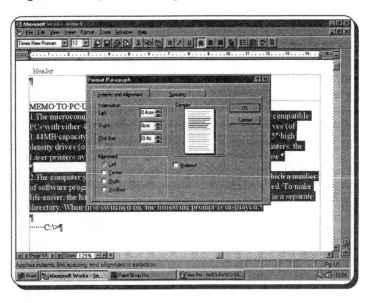

Most of the paragraph formatting operations can either be carried out from the Toolbar, or from this box. The alignment box offers:

Left	Smooth left edge, ragged right
Center	Text centred on line
Right	Smooth right edge, ragged left
Justified	Smooth left and right edges

To create left or right indents for the whole paragraph, type the amount of indent in the respective space, in centimetres.

If only the first line is to be indented, type the amount needed in the **First Line**, **Indents** space.

If you select the **Spacing** tab you will find options to fully control the spacing between lines and paragraphs. To keep a paragraph intact on one page, check the **Don't break paragraph** box. Select **Keep paragraph with next** to keep two paragraphs together on a page.

Hanging Indents:

The dialogue box on the previous page is set up to produce hanging indents, so that the paragraph numbers show up clearly at the left of the paragraphs.

To do this you should type the same value in the **First Line** box - with a negative sign in front - as that typed in the **Left**, **Indents** box. When you have finished, and saved the document as **Memo2**, your screen should look the same as that shown below.

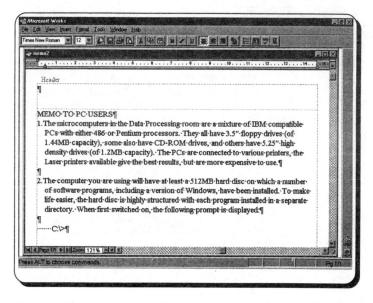

We will show you another way of creating hanging indents when we look at Easy Formats, on the next page.

Indenting with the Ruler:

If you look carefully at the Ruler at the top of the screen, after

you have placed an indent, you should see that an indent marker has been placed on it. This gives you another way of quickly setting and adjusting indents. You simply drag the marker to the new indent position, as shown by the drop down vertical line, and any selected paragraphs will be indented.

Easy Formats:

This is a feature new to Works for Windows 95 and is a simplified form of the Styles found in most fully fledged word processors.

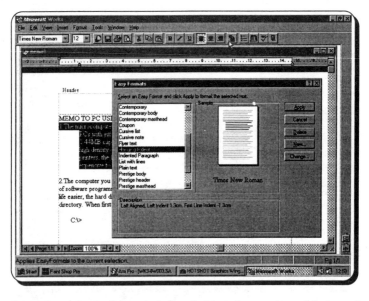

A range of useful pre-defined formats are provided and accessed by clicking the Easy Format Toolbar icon, or the **Format**, **Easy Formats** menu command.

In our example, on the facing page, we highlighted the first text paragraph of **Memo1** and selected the standard 'Hanging Indent' from the list shown in the dialogue box. To use the selected format you click the **Apply** button. You can also **Change** any of the standard formats provided, or create your own **New** ones.

This new feature allows you to standardise the formats you use for your documents, but it is a cumbersome procedure. The facility to 'paint' the formats, with the mouse pointer would be very useful.

Paragraph Borders:
As well as the Microsoft Draw and WordArt packages, which are described later, Works for Windows has the facility to place different types of lines, colours and shading patterns in and around selected paragraphs and pages, with the **Format, Borders and Shading** command. An example of the Border box and the results of its settings is shown below.

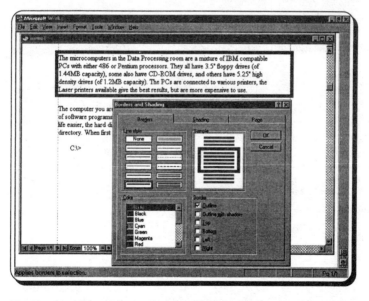

First, select the paragraphs you want to enhance, then in the Border box turn on the type of border you want, its **Line Style** and its **Color**, (not very English!) and then press

<Enter>, or select **OK**. To remove borders you must cancel the selections made in these boxes.

The Sample box will give you a good indication of how your borders, etc., will look. Even if you do not need these features very often, they are well worth exploring.

Printing Documents

Printers

When you installed Windows 95 your printers should have been installed as well. Over 800 different printers are supported by Windows 95 so, hopefully, you shouldn't have too much trouble getting yours to work. The printer and printing functions are now included in a single

Printers folder, which you can open by double-clicking the above icon in the My Computer window. Our Printers folder, shown on the right, has four printers available for use, and an Add Printer icon. This folder provides an easy way of adding new printers, configuring existing ones, and managing all your print jobs.

To 'manually' install a new printer to your set up, double-click the **Add Printer** icon in the Printers window. This opens the Windows 95 Add Printer Wizard, which really makes the installation procedure much easier than it used to be. As with all Wizards you progress from screen to screen by clicking the **Next** button. The first time

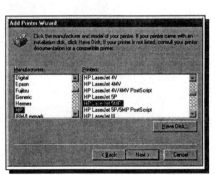

you do this, you have to wait a short time, while the printer driver information database is built.

The next dialogue box lets you choose the make and model of printer you want to install. In our case we are setting up a Hewlett Packard (HP in the list) model LaserJet 5MP. If you have a disc of drivers that came with the printer, put it in the floppy drive and click the **Have Disk** button.

You are next asked to select the correct Port. This refers to the socket at the back of your PC which is connected to the printer. For a stand alone set-up this would usually be the LPT1 port. (Short for Line Printer No.1). Next you can customise the printer name, maybe on a network, it would be useful to describe where it is actually located.

You should then accept **Yes** to have a test print carried out, to check that all is OK with the installation. When you click the **Finish** button a new icon will be placed in your Printers folder and, as long as the printer is switched on, a test page should be produced.

Hopefully, this test should give an impressive demonstration of the printer's capabilities and you will be able to answer **Yes** when asked if the test was successful. If not, click the **No** button, and Windows 95 will attempt to sort out the problem for you.

Configuring your Printer - All configuration for a printer is now consolidated onto a tabbed property sheet that is accessed from its icon in the Printers folder. Right clicking a printer icon opens the object menu, shown on the left, which gives control of

the printer's operation. If you click the **Properties** option, the dialogue box shown on the right opens and lets you control all the printer's parameters, such as the printer port (or network path), paper and graphics options, built in fonts, and other device options specific to the printer model. All these settings are fairly self explanatory and as they depend on your printer type we will let you work them out for yourselves.

If you use one printer all or most of the time, you should make it the default printer, by selecting **Set as Default** from its object (or right-click) menu. This saves continually having to select that printer from within your applications.

Now your printer is set up you can, at any time, use the **File, Print** command from the Works for Windows 95 document menu bar, or <Ctrl+P>, which both open the 'Print' box, shown below.

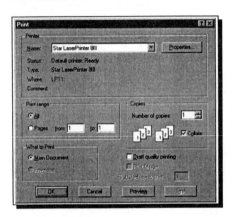

The settings in this box allow you to select which printer is used, the number of copies, and which pages are printed. **Draft quality printing** gives you a rapid hard copy, without fonts, enhancements or graphics. Finally select **OK**, to send print output from Works for Windows 95 to your selected destination, either the printer connected to your computer, or to an encoded file on disc.

The Print icon on the Toolbar sends the current document to the printer using the active settings. It does not give you access to the Print box.

Do remember that, whenever you change printers, the appearance of your document may change, as Works uses the fonts available with the newly selected printer. This can affect the line lengths, which in turn will affect both tabulation and pagination of your document.

Page Setup:

The next operation, to make sure your printer is happy with your document settings, is to set up Works for the paper and margin layout you want to use. The **File**, **Page Setup** command opens the tabbed dialogue box shown below. The settings in the three sections of this box are the UK default.

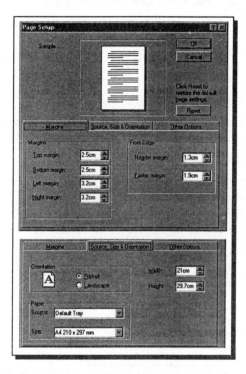

The **Margins** section includes settings for **Top, Bottom, Left** and **Right** margins, which are the non-print areas required on each edge of the paper. The **Header margin** is that required between the top of the page and the header line. The **Footer margin** is that between the bottom of the page and the footer line.

The **Source, Size and Orientation** section defaults to A4 size paper (210 x 297 mm). If you want to use a different size paper just select a standard size from the **Size** drop down list, or type in new dimensions for **Width** and **Height**. The default orientation is **Portrait** mode with the height of a page being greater than the width.

The **Other Options** section gives you control over the **Starting page number** which will normally be '1' unless you break up a piece of work into parts, or chapters, and of the printing of headers, footers and footnotes. These latter three are discussed later in this chapter.

Print Preview:

Works gives you an easy way of checking what your printer will produce with the **File**, **Print Preview** command. It lets you see a screen view of what the printed page should look like, similar to that shown below.

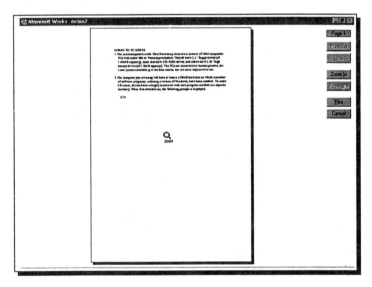

You can **Zoom In** or **Zoom Out,** or click the ZOOM mouse pointer over a section of the page, to see your work at different magnification levels, and step through a multi-page document with the **Previous** or **Next** buttons. If you are happy with the preview press **Print** to print the selected pages, otherwise press **Cancel** to exit Preview.

Text Enhancement

Tab Settings:

Works for Windows defaults to left aligned tabs every 1.3cm, or 0.5in, across the page. For most purposes these will be adequate, but if you need to generate lists, or tables, indexes, etc., the custom tab facility should prove useful. There are four types of custom tab stops:

Left	Text aligns to the right of tab
Right	Text aligns to the left of tab
Center	Text centres on tab stop
Decimal	Text aligns at a decimal point

Tabs are shown on the ruler at the top of the screen, as can be seen below.

All default tabs to the left of a new custom tab are removed automatically. You can also select one of four types of leader characters to fill the space to the tab spot. This is useful when preparing contents pages.

The example below shows part of a contents page which has two **Left** aligned tabs for the subjects, and a **Right** tab with a dot leader for the page numbers. To set custom tab

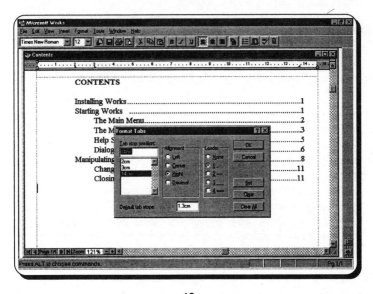

stops, select the required paragraph, or the whole document, and either double click your mouse on the ruler, or choose **Format, Tabs**. A dialogue box like the one shown on the previous page will open.

If necessary, type the **Tab stop position** in the text box, select the options needed from the **Alignment** and **Leader** boxes and choose **Set** to place the tab on the ruler. This operation can be repeated for as many tabs as are required. Use the **Clear**, or **Clear All** buttons to remove one tab, or all the tabs, from the ruler.

Tables of figures can be created, and adjusted, by the careful use of tab settings. Use decimal, or right aligned tab stops, for columns of figures. It is an easy matter to readjust the width of columns by resetting the tabs, even after the table has been created.

The Tables feature, discussed later in the chapter, is an easier way of creating such tables however.

Headers and Footers:

In a printed document a header is text that appears at the top of each page of the document, whilst a footer appears at the bottom. These can be used to add page numbers, titles, dates and times to your documents.

These are easily added in page view mode by simply typing text, and embedding code, in the WYSIWYG Header and Footer boxes at the top and bottom of the screen page.

A header is shown in the next example on the facing page. This can be added to the file **Memo2**, in Page View mode as follows.

Move the cursor to the start of the header box and add the date special command, using either <Ctrl+D>, or the **Insert**, **Date and Time** menu command. With the latter you can choose the format of the date. This adds today's date to the screen, but will print the current date on paper. Press <Tab> and the cursor is automatically centred on the line. Add a title and press <Tab> again to bring the cursor to the right hand side of the page. Type 'Page ' followed by the **Insert**, **Page Number** command, which will embed the *page* code on the screen, but will print the page number, and save as **Memo3**.

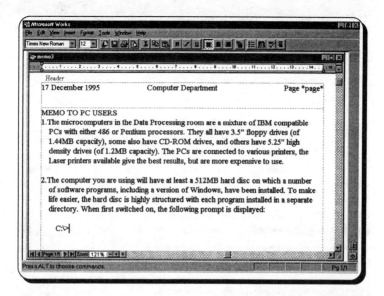

Your screen should now look like that shown above. Use the **File**, **Print Preview** command to quickly check the printed result. If you want, you can add enhancements, or change the fonts of the header and footer text.

Footnotes:

A useful feature in Works for Windows 95 is the ability to place reference marks, or numbers, anywhere in a document. Text can be 'attached' to each reference, which will automatically be printed at the end of the relevant page. This operation is carried out with the **Insert**, **Footnote** command.

Footnotes are automatically numbered, and renumbered if edited, but you can also specify other reference marks (such as * or $, for example).

To create a footnote, move the cursor to the position in the

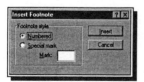

document where the reference mark is needed, choose **Insert**, **Footnote,** alter the dialogue box if you want to force a mark instead of a numbered reference, and select **Insert**.

51

If **Numbered** is selected in the box, the next consecutive footnote number is placed at the cursor and the footnote pane is opened at the bottom of the page. Type the reference text here, and format, or enhance it, if required. You move the cursor back to the document with the mouse when you are ready.

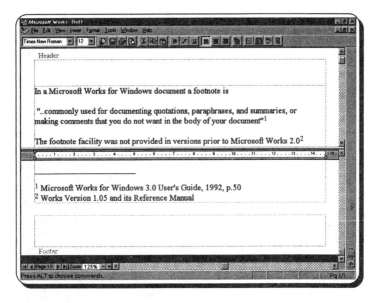

Our example above shows two footnotes placed in the body text, and the note text in a split window at the bottom of the page.

Once placed, footnote reference marks are always shown in the document. Footnote text can be edited, the same as any other text and reference marks can also be moved, copied or deleted, with Works looking after the positioning of the attached text.

Endnotes:

When you print a document that contains footnotes, they are placed at the bottom of the page holding the reference point. To force your reference text to be printed at the end of the main body of the document text, place them as described above, but check the **File**, **Page Setup**, **Other Options**, **Print footnotes at end** option.

Your final printed presentation of these endnotes will be improved if you place blank lines at the end of your document text. Without these the footnote text will be printed immediately under the last line of document text. Any reference heading required should then be placed after these blank lines.

Searching for and Replacing Text:

Works allows you to search for specifically selected text, or character combinations. In the search mode, actioned with the **Edit**, **Find** command, it will highlight each occurrence in turn so that you can carry out some action on it, such as change its font or appearance.

In the **Edit**, **Replace** mode you specify what replacement is to be automatically carried out. For example, in a long book

chapter you may decide to replace every occurrence of the word 'programme' with the word 'program'. This is very easy to do. First go to the beginning of the file, as search only operates in a forward direction, then choose **Edit**, **Replace**. In the **Find what** box, type **programme**, and in the **Replace with** box type **program**. To make sure that part words are not selected, choose the **Find whole words only** option, and then click the **Find Next** button. The first match will be highlighted in the document then either choose **Replace**, to change once, or **Replace All** for automatic replacement.

Works automatically matches the capitalisation of any text it replaces. If the replaced word is at the beginning of a sentence it will capitalise the first letter. If you select the **Match case** option, only text with the exactly specified case letters will be selected.

You can search for, and replace, special characters, or a combination of text and special characters (for example, tab or paragraph marks, or white space). White space is a combination of any number of consecutive spaces and tab marks. A very useful example of this is when you have imported columnar data from another file, and the columns are separated with spaces; you can search for white space, and replace it with a tab, to realign the columns.

Another example would be searching for a word, which occurs at the beginning of a paragraph, or after a tab. Two special characters, tab and the paragraph marker, have icons placed in the Find and Replace dialogue boxes. Clicking these, places their mark in the selected text box. The list below also gives the key combinations of these and the other special characters to enable them to be entered into Find and Replace boxes.

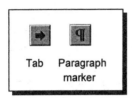

Tab   Paragraph
          marker

To type the caret (^) character, press <Shift+6>.

To search for, or replace	*Type*
Tab mark	^t
Paragraph mark	^p
End-of-line mark	^n
Page break mark	^d
Non-breaking space	^s
Caret (^)	^^
Question mark (?)	^?
White space	^w
Any character (wild card)	?

Using the Spell Checker:

If you have a problem with spelling, the spell checker in Works for Windows 95 will be a popular part of the package! It will search for wrongly spelled words, words with incorrect capitalisation, incorrect hyphenation, and repeated words, such as 'if if'. It has a large built-in dictionary, and you can add other words that you may need to check for in the future.

To check the spelling of a whole document, move the cursor to the beginning with <Ctrl+Home>. Alternatively, you can select the text you want checked. In either case, invoke the checker by choosing **Tools**, **Spelling**, with the **F7** key, or by clicking the Spelling Checker icon. When a word that is not recognised is found, a box appears as shown in the example below.

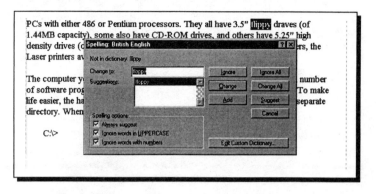

A problem message will appear in the top left corner of the box, the suspect word will be highlighted in the document, and will also be placed in the **Change to** box.

You have several options now:

a. To leave the word unchanged choose **Ignore** for this occurrence, or **Ignore All**.

b. To change the word, edit, or re-type it, in the box, and choose **Change**, or **Change All** to change all instances of that word in the document.

c. Choose **Suggest**, to view a list of proposed spellings from the dictionary, select one and then choose **Change**.

d. To add an edited word to the dictionary, choose **Add**.

When you have made your choice, the program continues searching the rest of the document. To leave the checker at any time simply choose **Cancel**. We found the Spell Checker to be much faster, and surprisingly, more accurate than the one with the previous version of Works for Windows.

Using the Thesaurus:

To help you with composing your documents Works has a built-in thesaurus. With this you should be able to find a synonym, or word with a similar meaning, for most words. First select the word you want to change, and choose **Tools**, **Thesaurus**, or press the <Shift+F7> keys. This opens the dialogue box shown below.

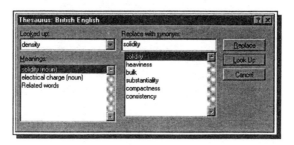

In the **Meanings** box, on the left, are suggestions of the main meanings of the selected word. Depending on the context in the document, you need to select one of these meanings, and then look in the **Replace with synonym** box for a list of possible replacement words.

In the example shown 'density' was the word highlighted in the document. The noun 'solidity' was selected from the **Meanings** list which produced the five synonyms shown. Sometimes the logic of the choices has to make you smile.

If you select one of the synonyms and press **Look Up** you should get more alternatives to look at.

To replace the original word highlighted in your document, select the best alternative and choose **Replace**.

Word Count:

Works for Windows 95 includes the facility to count the words in a document, or block of selected text. This can be useful if you are working on an assignment that requires a specific number of words. The program considers a word to be any text between two space characters. Select the text to be counted and use the **Tools**, **Word Count** command. If no text is selected the whole document will be counted, including footnotes, headers and footers.

Adding a Note to your Document

A very useful, if rather 'flamboyant', facility added to Works for Windows is the ability to add 'pop-up' notes anywhere in your documents. Place the cursor where you want a Note to be placed and action the **Insert**, **Note-It** command. The following dialogue box is opened.

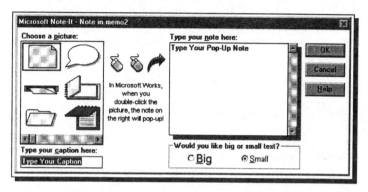

The **Choose a picture** box gives you the amazing choice of 58 different note types. If it turns you on, you can liven up your document no end! To place a caption under the displayed note, type the required text in the **Type your caption here** text box. The main text to be 'hidden' in the note is typed in the **Type your note here** box. Select the size of Note text you want from the **Big** and **Small** options and finally press **OK** to place your note.

At any time in the future the note text can be read by double clicking on the note, as shown in the example on the next page.

The size of the Note icon in our example was reduced after it was placed, by first selecting the Note graphic (by clicking it) and entering 50% in both the **Height** and **Width**, **Scaling** options of the **Format**, **Picture** box.

Notes can be very useful if several people are editing a document and they want to make comments for the others to see. Each person would then choose a different shape of note icon, which would be recognisable by the rest of the team.

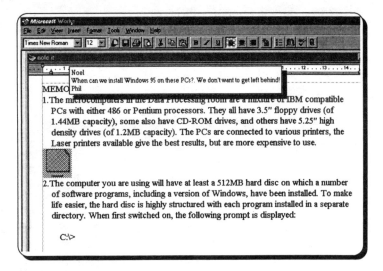

Adding WordArt to your Document

The WordArt facility lets you easily create quite eye-catching title lines for your documents. To use it, place the insertion point where you want the heading and use the **Insert**, **WordArt** command. Type your heading text and note that a new Toolbar has been added to the screen, as shown below.

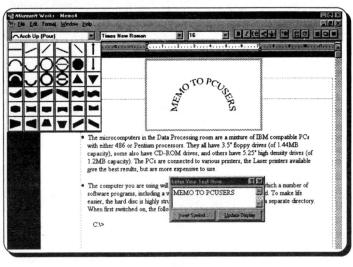

This also shows the shapes available in the drop down menu
opened on the left of the bar. The buttons on the Toolbar are
used to design the look of your WordArt text, as follows:

Click	*To*
Plain Text	Choose a shape for WordArt
Arial	Change the font
Best Fit	Change the font size
B	Make text bold
I	Make text italic
EE	Make letters all the same height, regardless of their capitalisation
	Flip letters on their side
	Stretch text to the edges of the frame
	Choose how text aligns in a frame
	Change the spacing between letters
	Adjust the shape of the text, or rotate text within a frame
	Change the colour or shading of text
	Add a shadow to text
	Add a border to text

When your heading looks the way you want, simply click the
pointer outside the dialogue box to return to your document,
which should now have the new heading placed on it. You
can edit a WordArt graphic at any time by double-clicking it.

To change the position of a WordArt feature, or any other Works graphic, select it and use the **Format**, **Picture**, **Text Wrap**, **Absolute** command and then you can drag it around the page.

Adding a Drawing to a Document

It is a very easy matter to add a ClipArt drawing to your documents. Works comes with a folder (or more) of professional graphics for you to use. They are added with the **Insert**, **ClipArt** command, which opens the Microsoft ClipArt Gallery shown below.

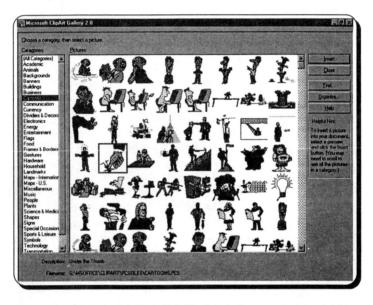

This even includes a **Helpful Hint** to tell you what to do! You can add more images to the Gallery, and change categories, etc., in the **Organise** box.

It is also possible to Paste a graphic from the Windows clipboard into your document. It will be placed, as with ClipArt, into its own frame.

Once your graphic is placed in the document and selected (by clicking it), you can move, copy, Drag and Drop and delete it the same as you can with selected text. You can also re-size it.

You may, however, need to set **Text Wrap**, as **Absolute** as described on the last page, or the graphic will only flow with its surrounding text.

Adding a Table to a Document

The ability to use 'Tables' is built into most top-range word processors these days. Works for Windows 95 has an excellent one built into the word processor.

Tables are used to create adjacent columns of text and numeric data. A table is simply a grid of columns and rows with the intersection of a column and row forming a rectangular box referred to as a 'cell'. Data is placed into individual cells that are organised into columns and rows, similar to a spreadsheet. You can modify the appearance of table data by applying text formatting and enhancements.

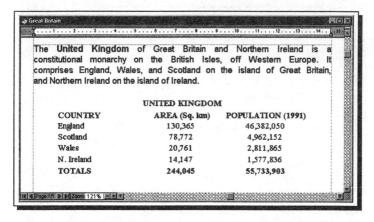

The United Kingdom of Great Britain and Northern Ireland is a constitutional monarchy on the British Isles, off Western Europe. It comprises England, Wales, and Scotland on the island of Great Britain, and Northern Ireland on the island of Ireland.

UNITED KINGDOM

COUNTRY	AREA (Sq. km)	POPULATION (1991)
England	130,365	46,382,050
Scotland	78,772	4,962,152
Wales	20,761	2,811,865
N. Ireland	14,147	1,577,836
TOTALS	244,045	55,733,903

As an example we will step through the process of creating the table shown above. To build this geographical, but non-political, example place the insertion point after the document body text and use the **Insert**, **Table** command.

In the opened dialogue box enter 7 as the **Number of rows** and leave the **Number of columns** as 3. There are 28 different table formats to choose from, we used the 'Plain' one as a starter. When you are happy with the procedures we suggest you experiment with the other formats.

Pressing **OK** returns you to your document in which a full width table has been placed. To see the cells in the table, as shown below, toggle the **View**, **Gridlines** command.

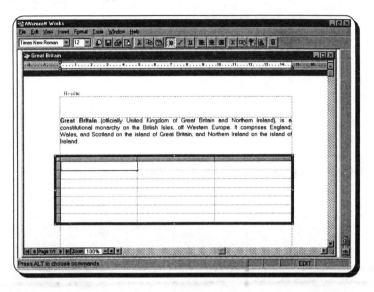

Note that the Toolbar has four new icons when a table is selected, and that the menu bar options are also changed.

If you click your document outside the empty table just the gridlines will show. Single clicking in the table will partly select it and place grey 'handles' around the border. These

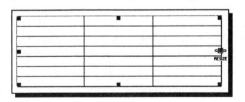

allow you to re-size the table, by dragging the RESIZE pointer with the left mouse button depressed, as shown here.

When the table is selected like this you can also set its alignment on the page with the Toolbar icons. Ours was centred in this way.

Double-clicking in the table will fully select it and place the solid border around its edge.

In our example the table title is centred across the top. To do this move the pointer over the border next to the top left cell, until it changes to a hollow cross, as shown below. Clicking

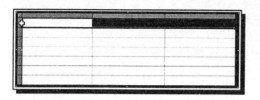

now will select the whole of the top row. Now right click in the selected area and select **Format** from the object menu that opens. Select **Alignment**, **Center across cells** from the very powerful Format Cells dialogue box that is opened, and then type the table title in the centred top row.

Enter the other data as shown, but not the actual totals at this stage. To format the column titles you can select the whole of the second row and click the Bold and Centre Align Toolbar icons.

By default, entered numbers show right aligned and with no commas. To re-format them, highlight all the number cells and from the **Number** tab of the Format Cells dialogue box select the **Comma** format with no **Decimal places**. Clicking **OK** will change them straight away.

The totals on the bottom line could just be typed in, once they were calculated. But with Tables you don't need to use your calculator, Works will do this for you automatically. Select the 'Area Total' cell and click the AutoSum Toolbar icon, as shown below.

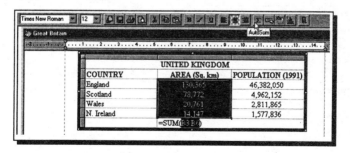

This highlights the column figures and places a spreadsheet formula as shown. Press <Enter> to accept it.

63

	A	B	C
1			
2			
3		▓	

Works performs mathematical calculations on numbers in cells, but uses their addresses in its formulae. Cells are referred to as A1, A2, B1, B2, and so on, with the letter representing a column and the number representing a row. Thus, B3 refers to the hatched cell, in this example.

Complete the table now by copying the formula in cell C6 to the 'Population Total' cell, C7. The Copy and Paste Toolbar icons are the easiest ways to do this.

Format any data that needs it and finally turn off the gridlines, as the printed table looks better without them.

This is only a simple example of the power and features of Works Tables. A Table can use almost all the features that are available to you in the Spreadsheet tool.

4. MICROSOFT DRAW

The Drawing Tool

Works for Windows 95 also includes Microsoft Draw, a quite comprehensive drawing and graphics manipulation package. This is actually a separate program which can be accessed from the Works word processing tool. You can import existing drawings into a document with the Microsoft Draw tool, which can also be used to create, or edit, drawings consisting of lines, arcs, ellipses, text and rectangles. The Draw tool is opened by either using the **Drawing** option from the **Insert** menu of the Word Processor, or double-clicking within an existing picture in a document. When opened from the menu, the drawing tool runs in a separate window, as shown below. When it is closed any graphics created will be embedded in the document at the cursor position.

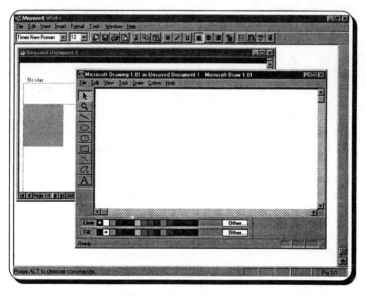

Microsoft Draw is an OLE (object linking and embedding, and pronounced 'Oh-lay') type of Windows program.

The Draw Help system is quite detailed, as shown in the package overview on the next page.

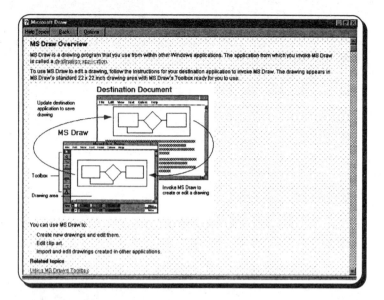

Using the Microsoft Draw tool, you can create and select objects in a picture, then copy and move them, or change their size, shape and colour, etc. These options can be carried out either by using the toolbar on the left of the Draw screen, or by using the Draw pull-down menus.

Using the Draw Toolbar:

Works provides a variety of buttons in the Toolbar on the left of the Draw screen, both for creating objects such as lines, circles, squares, or text objects and for manipulating these objects, once they have been selected. The buttons on the Draw toolbar are:

 Selection Arrow - Selects or sizes an object, or group of objects.

 Magnifying Glass - Selects a specified area of a picture and magnifies it.

 Line - Draws a straight line in the direction you drag the mouse. To draw a line at a perfect 45 degree angle, hold <Shift> while dragging the mouse.

66

Ellipse - Draws an ellipse. To draw a circle, hold <Shift> while dragging the mouse.

Rounded Rectangle - Draws a rectangle with rounded corners. To draw a rounded square, hold <Shift> and drag the mouse.

Rectangle - Draws a rectangle. To draw a square, hold <Shift> and drag the mouse.

Arc - Draws an arc. You can create a Bezier curve by modifying an arc.

Freehand/Polygon - Draws freehand lines, or draws polygons. When you finish, press <Esc>.

Text - Places the insertion point inside a drawing so you can type text, each paragraph of which will become an object, which you can then manipulate.

Draw Menu Commands:

Most of the menu commands available with Microsoft Draw are self-explanatory. The few that are not, are listed below with details of their function.

Command	*Function*
File, Update	Updates the drawing in the Works for Windows document.
File, Import Picture	Loads a graphic file from disc to the Draw package.
File, Exit & Return	Closes Draw and returns control to Works for Windows.
Draw, Group	Groups the selected objects.
Draw, Ungroup	Ungroups the selected objects.
Draw, Framed	Draws an outline frame around the selected object.

67

Draw, **F**illed	Changes the fill pattern of the selected object to the current fill pattern.
Draw, **P**attern	Displays colour and fill pattern options.
Draw, **L**ine Style	Displays line styles available and thickness of lines.
Draw, Snap to G**r**id	Aligns objects automatically, or manually, on the grid.
Draw, Sho**w** Guides	Displays vertical and horizontal guide lines.
Draw, R**o**tate/Flip	Rotates/flips the selected object, or group of objects, clockwise or anticlockwise.

Creating a Drawing:

To create an object, click on the required Draw button, such as the ellipse, position the mouse pointer where you want to create the object on the screen, and then drag the mouse to draw the object. Hold the <Shift> key while you drag the mouse to create a perfect circle, square, or rounded square. If you do not hold <Shift>, Draw creates an ellipse, a rectangle, or a rounded rectangle.

You can use the freehand/polygon Draw button to create freehand objects. First click on the freehand button, then position the mouse pointer where you want to create the object on the screen. If you then press the left mouse button and keep it pressed, the mouse pointer changes to the shape of a pencil with which you can draw freehand. If, on the other hand, you click the left mouse button, the edge of the line attaches itself on the drawing area, at the point of contact, and the pointer changes to a crosshair. A straight line can then be drawn between that point and the next point on which you happen to click the mouse button. In this way you can draw polygons. When you finish drawing with either of these two methods, press the <Esc> key.

Editing a Drawing:

To **select** an object, first click the 'Selection Arrow' button and then click the desired object. Draw displays black handles around the object selected.

You can **move** an object, or multiple objects, within a drawing by selecting them and dragging them to the desired position.

To **copy** an object, click at the object, then use the **Edit, Copy** / **Edit, Paste** commands.

To **size** an object within Draw, position the mouse pointer on a black handle and then drag the handle until the object is the desired shape and size.

To **delete** an object, select the object and press <Del>. To delete a drawing, hold the <Shift> key down and click each object in turn that makes up the drawing, then press <Del>. You could also use instead the **Edit, Select All** command, and then press the <Del> key.

Using Layered Drawings:

You can use Draw's **Edit**, **Bring to Front** or **Send to Back** commands to determine the order of layered drawings. Drawings or pictures layered on top of each other can create useful visual effects, provided you remember that the top drawing/picture obscures the one below it.

Using Line and Fill:

You can use the 'Line' and 'Fill' colour palette at the bottom of Draw's screen, to specify the colour of the lines and the colour of the fill pattern for selected drawings/pictures. The first time you access Microsoft Draw, the line colour is black and the fill pattern is transparent.

We will leave it up to you to find practical uses for all the above features of the Draw package. Have fun.

5. THE WORKS SPREADSHEET

When you first enter the Works for Windows 95 spreadsheet, the program sets up a huge electronic page, or worksheet, in your computer's memory, many times larger than the small part shown on the screen. Individual cells are identified by column and row location (in that order), with the present size extending to 256 columns by a massive 16,384 rows. The columns are labelled from A to Z, followed by AA to AZ, BA to BZ, and so on, to IV, while the rows are numbered from 1 to 16,384.

Using the Works Task Launcher and selecting the **Spreadsheet** option from the **Works Tools** dialogue box, displays the following spreadsheet screen:

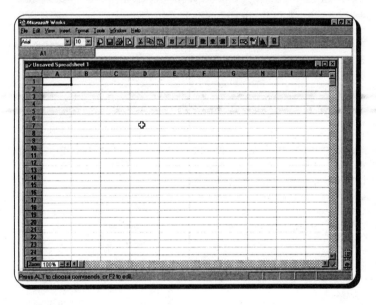

A spreadsheet can be thought of as a two-dimensional table made up of rows and columns. The point where a row and column intersect is called a cell, while the reference points of a cell are known as the cell address. The active cell (A1 when you first enter the program) is highlighted.

Worksheet Navigation

Navigation around the worksheet is achieved by the use of the four arrow keys. Each time one of these keys is pressed, the active cell moves one position right, down, left or up, depending on which arrow key was pressed. The <PgDn> and <PgUp> keys can also be used to move vertically one full page at a time, while the <Ctrl+PgDn> and <Ctrl+PgUp> key combinations can be used to move horizontally one full page at a time. Pressing the arrow keys while holding down the <Ctrl> key causes the active cell to be moved to the extremities of the worksheet. For example, <Ctrl+→> moves the active cell to the IV column, while <Ctrl+↓> moves the active cell to the 16,384th row.

You can move the active cell with a mouse by moving the mouse pointer to the cell you want to activate and clicking the left mouse button. If the cell is not visible, then move the window by clicking on the scroll bar arrowhead that points in the direction you want to move, until the cell you want to activate is visible. To move a page at a time, click in the scroll bar itself, or for larger moves, drag the scroll box in the scroll bar.

When you have finished navigating around the worksheet, press the <Ctrl+Home> keys which will move the active cell to the A1 position. This is known as the 'Home' position. If you press the <Home> key by itself, the active cell is moved to the 1st column of the particular row. Note that there are several areas on your screen; the displayed area within which you can move the active cell is referred to as the working area of the worksheet, while the letters and numbers in the border around the displayed portion of the worksheet form the reference points.

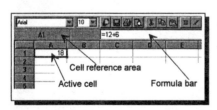

The location of the active cell is constantly monitored in the Cell Reference Area at the left end of the Formula Bar, below the Toolbar. If you type text in the active cell, what you type appears both in the formula bar and in the cell itself. Typing a formula which is preceded by the equals sign (=) to, say, add the contents of two cells, causes the actual formula to appear in the 'formula bar', while the result of the actual calculation appears in the active cell when the <Enter> key is pressed.

The GOTO Command:

Sometimes it is necessary to move to a specific address in the worksheet which, however, is so far from your present position that using the arrow keys might take far too long to get there. To this end, Works has implemented the **F5** function key as a 'go to' command. For example, to jump to position HZ4000, press the **F5** key, which will cause Works to ask for the address of the cell to which it is to jump. This request appears in a dialogue box.

Now, typing HZ4000 and pressing <Enter>, causes the active cell to jump to that cell address. To specify a cell address, you must always key one or two letters followed by a number. The letters can range from A to IV corresponding to a column, while the numbers can range from 1 to 16,384 corresponding to a row. Specifying a column or row outside this range will cause an error message to be displayed in the dialogue box. To clear the error, press <Enter>, or the <Esc> key; the <Esc> key can also be used to cancel a command and escape from a situation before an error occurs.

Entering Information

We will now investigate how information can be entered into the worksheet. But first, return to the Home (A1) position by pressing <Ctrl+Home>, then type in the words:

```
PROJECT ANALYSIS
```

As you type, the characters appear in both the 'formula bar' and the active cell window.

If you make a mistake, press the <BkSp> key to erase the previous letter or the <Esc> key to start again. When you have finished, press <Enter>. Note that what you have just typed in has been entered in cell A1, even though part of the word ANALYSIS appears to be in cell B1. If you use the right arrow key to move the active cell to B1 you will see that the cell is indeed empty.

Note that the text displayed in the 'formula bar' is prefixed by double quotation marks (") which were added automatically by the program to indicate that the entry is a 'label' and not a number, or a date. Thus, typing a letter at the beginning of an entry into a cell results in a 'label' being formed. If the length of a label is longer than the width of a cell, it will continue into the next cell to the right of the current active cell, provided that cell is empty, otherwise the displayed label will be truncated.

To edit information already in a cell, move the pointer to the appropriate cell and either press the **F2** function key, or click in the 'formula bar'. The cursor keys, the <Home> and <End> keys, as well as the <Ins> and <Del> keys can be used to move the cursor and/or edit the information displayed in the 'formula bar', as required. After such editing of information in the formula bar, you must either press the <Enter> key, or click the '√' button on the formula bar, to enter it in the active cell.

Now use the arrow keys to move the active cell to B3 and type

```
"Jan
```

Then press the right-arrow key, which will automatically enter the abbreviation 'Jan' into the cell, as a label, and will also move the active cell to position C3. Had we only typed Jan (without the double quotes prefix) on pressing either <Enter> or the right-arrow key, the word 'January' would have appeared automatically in the cell, as a date. In cell C3, type

```
"Feb
```

and again press the right-arrow key.

The looks of a worksheet can be enhanced considerably by placing lines, or cell borders, to separate information in different rows. Select the cells A4 to C4 (from the keyboard use the <Shift+→> keystroke; with the mouse drag the active cell) and choose the **Format**, **Border** menu command. This opens the Border tabbed section of the Format Cells dialogue box, from which you can place any combination of lines along the borders of selected cells. In our case, select **Top** and the heavy **Line style** option and press **OK** to accept the settings.

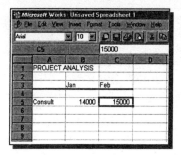

Finally, type in the label and amounts earned in columns A, B and C of row 5, as shown in the screen dump alongside.

Note how the labels 'Jan' and 'Feb' do not appear above the numbers 14000 and 15000. This is because by default, labels are left justified, while numbers are right justified.

Changing Text Alignment and Fonts:

One way of improving the looks of this worksheet is to also right justify the labels 'Jan' and 'Feb' within their respective cells. To do this, move the active cell to B3 and mark the range B3 to C3 (from the keyboard use the <Shift+→> keystroke; with the mouse drag the active cell), choose the **Format, Alignment** command, then select the **Right** option listed in the Alignment tabbed section of the Format Cells dialogue box and press <Enter>. The labels should now appear right justified within their cells. An easier way to carry out this operation is to select the cells and click the Right Align Toolbar icon, shown here.

We could further improve the looks of the worksheet by choosing a different font for the heading 'Project Analysis'. To achieve this, move the active cell to A1, choose the **Format, Font and Style** command, then select Courier New, **Size** 8 and **Italic**, from the options listed in the displayed dialogue box, and press **OK**. The heading will now appear in Courier New 8, Italic font.

Once again the Toolbar gives a much quicker way of carrying out these operations. Simply click the down arrow alongside the Font Name or Font Size icons, shown above, and make your selection from the menus that drop down.

Finally, since the entered numbers in cells B5 to C5 represent money, it would be better if these were displayed with two digits after the decimal point and prefixed with the £ sign. To do this, move the active cell to B5 and select the cell block B5 to C5, then choose the **Format**, **Number, Currency** command and accept the default number of decimals, which is 2. This formatting operation can also be done by clicking the Currency Toolbar icon, shown here, which formats selected cells to currency with 2 decimal places. The numbers within the marked worksheet range should now be displayed in the new format. If the width of the relevant cells had not been large enough to accommodate all the digits of the new format, they would have been filled with the hash character (#) to indicate insufficient space. The columns would then need to be widened.

Changing the Column Width:

To change the width of a given column or a number of columns, activate a cell in the relevant column, or block the number of required column cells, use the **Format** command and select the **Column Width** option from the pull-down sub-menu. This causes a dialogue box to be displayed with the **Standard** column width offered as 10 characters, or a **Best Fit** option which ensures all entries in the column fit. Typing 12 and pressing <Enter>, changes the width of the selected columns to 12 characters.

A quicker method of doing this, if you prefer, is to position

	A	B	C	D
	PROJECT ANALYSIS		ADJUST	
		Jan	Feb	
Consult	£14,000.00	####		

the mouse pointer in the column headings at the top of the working area. It will change shape as you move it over the border of two columns. Dragging this new pointer right or left, will widen, or narrow, the column to the left.

If the currency symbol displays as a '$' don't panic, it just means your version of Windows 95 is not set up for the UK. To remedy this open the Control Panel by clicking the **Start** button on the

Windows 95 TaskBar, followed by **Settings**, **Control Panel**.
Double-click on the Regional Settings icon. Make sure that
English (British) is selected on the opening tabbed page. The
Currency page settings should then be correct, as shown
below, if not simply change them.

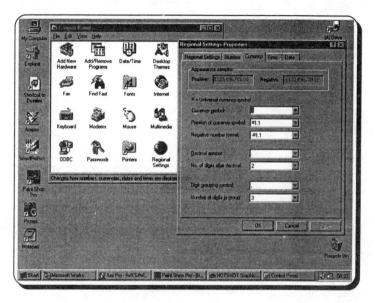

You can, of course, customise these Regional settings for
wherever on the globe you happen to be.

Now change the contents of cell A5 from 'Consult' to
'Consultancy'.

Saving a Worksheet

At this point, you might like to stop entering information in
your worksheet, and save the work so far carried out, before
leaving the program. You can do this by choosing the **File,
Save** command which, when used for the first time with a file,
opens the Save As dialogue box.

For our exercise, type the **File name** as **Project1** and
press <Enter>, or click the **Save** button (the extension .WKS
will be added by Works). If you prefer to save your work on a
floppy disc in, say, the A: drive, instead of in the Documents
folder, you could make your selection in the **Save in** box.

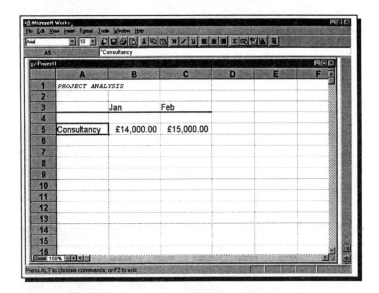

What you should see displayed on your screen after the above commands have been issued, is shown above, at a zoom factor of 150% for clarity.

At this point you could exit Works for Windows 95 and switch off your computer, safe in the knowledge that your work is saved on disc and can be retrieved at any time.

Exiting Works for Windows:

To exit Works, either click the Application X Close button, use the **File, Exit Works** command, or the <Alt+**F4**> keys. If you have made any changes to your work since the last time you saved it, an alert box will be displayed on your screen to ask you if you would like to save the file before leaving the program.

Filling in a Worksheet

We will use, as an example of how a spreadsheet can be built up, the few entries on 'Project Analysis' which we used previously. If you haven't saved the **Project1** example, don't worry as you could just as easily start afresh.

Retrieving a Worksheet:

If you have saved **Project1**, then enter the Works program, and choose **Existing Documents** from the Task Launcher. A list of recently used documents should be shown. Highlighting one of these will show its full path immediately below the list, as shown in our example below.

To retrieve other documents that are not listed, click the **Open a document not listed here** 'waffle-like' button and open its location folder. If you don't know the document's actual location on your system, try using the **Help me find a document** button. When you have selected the file you want, in our case, **Project1**, click **OK** to open it.

A quick way to retrieve one of the last files used by Works is to open the **File** menu and click on the file's name at the bottom of the menu options. As you highlight the files in this list their full path locations are shown on the status bar.

When the file is open, use the **F2** function key to 'Edit' the existing entries, or simply retype the contents of cells (see the next section for the formatting of the example) so that your worksheet looks like the one on the next page.

Formatting Entries:

Because of the length of some of the labels used and the formatting of the numbers, the default widths of cells in our worksheet were changed from the existing 10 to 12. If you haven't done this already, mark the cell block A1:E1, and choose the **F**ormat, **Column Width** command, and type 12 for the new width of the cells.

The information in cell A1

```
PROJECT ANALYSIS: ADEPT CONSULTANTS LTD
```

was entered left justified and formatted by choosing the Courier New, size 12, Italic Toolbar icons. The labels in the cell block B3-E3 were formatted with the Right Align icon, so they are displayed right justified.

The numbers within the cell block B5-E17 were formatted by clicking the Currency icon, which defaulted to two decimal places. All the labels appearing in column A (apart from that in cell A1) were just typed in (left justified), as shown.

The lines in cells A4 to E4 and A14 to E14 were entered using the **F**ormat, **B**order command and selecting **T**op. Those in cells A6 to E6 and A16 to E16 were entered using **F**ormat, **B**order and selecting **B**ottom.

80

Entering Text, Numbers and Formulae:

When text, numbers or formulae are entered into a cell, or reference is made to the contents of a cell by the cell address, or a Works for Windows function is entered into a cell, then the content of the message line changes from 'Press ALT to choose commands, or F2 to edit' to 'Press ENTER, or ESC to cancel'. This message can be changed back to the former one either by completing an entry and pressing <Enter> or one of the arrow keys, or by pressing the <Esc> key.

In our example, we can find the 1st quarter total income from consultancy, by activating cell E5 and typing the formula

    =B5+C5+D5

followed by <Enter>. The total first quarter consultancy income is added, using this formula, and the result is placed in cell E5. Note, however, that when cell E5 is activated, the 'formula bar' displays the actual formula used to calculate the contents of the cell.

Complete the insertion into the spreadsheet of the various amounts under 'costs' and then choose the **File, Save As** command to save the resultant worksheet under the filename **Project2**, before going on any further. Remember that saving your work on disc often is a good policy to get used to, as even the shortest power cut can cause the loss of hours of hard work!

Using Functions

In our example, writing a formula that adds the contents of three columns is not too difficult or lengthy a task. But imagine having to add 20 columns the same way! For this reason Works, like all spreadsheets, has an in-built summation function (for the many others see Appendix A) in the form of =SUM( ) which can be used to add any number of columns (or rows).

To illustrate how this function can be used, activate cell E5 and type

    =SUM(

then use the mouse pointer to highlight the cells in the summation range (B5 to D5 in this case).

What appears against the cell indicator is the entry

```
SUM(B5:D5
```

which has to be completed by typing the closing parenthesis (round bracket) and pressing <Enter>.

The Autosum Function:

Another clever feature in Works is the facility to automatically enter the above =SUM() function into the worksheet. To automatically sum a series of numbers in either a column, or a row, place the active cell below the column, or to the right of the row, and click the Autosum Toolbar icon, shown here, or press the <Ctrl+M> quick key combination. Works enters the formula for you; all you have to do is press <Enter>, or click the Enter button (✓) on the Formula bar, to accept it.

Easy Calc:

A new feature in Works for Windows 95 is Easy Calc, which helps you add functions to your spreadsheets. To use it, place the active cell where you want to add a function (cell E8 in our example) and click the Easy Calc Toolbar icon shown here. If you prefer, use the **Tools**, **Easy Calc** menu command. Both open the dialogue box shown on the left below, which should help to enter the correct function for your needs. Clicking **Sum** opens the box shown on the right.

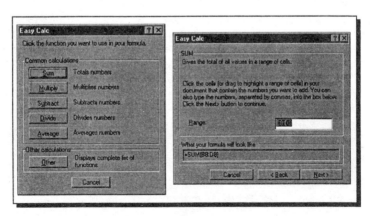

Copying Cell Contents:

To copy information into other cells we could repeat the above procedure (in this particular case entering the SUM() function in each cell within the cell range E8 through E13), or we could choose the **Edit**, **Copy** command, point to the cell we would like to copy information into and **Paste** it.

To illustrate the copy command, activate cell E5 and click the Copy icon, or choose the **Edit**, **Copy** command, or press <Ctrl+C>, which copies the cell contents to the Windows clipboard. Move the highlighted cell to E8 and click the Paste icon, or press **Edit**, **Paste**, or the <Ctrl+V> quick key. Then, block the cell range E8:E13 (by either using the <Shift+↓> keystroke or dragging the mouse) and choose the **Edit, Fill Down** command.

Immediately this command is chosen the actual sums of the 'relative' columns appear in the target area. Notice that when you activate cell E5, the function target range is B5:D5, while when you activate cell E8 the function target range changes to B8:D8 which indicates that copying formulae with this method causes the 'relative' target range to be copied. Had the 'absolute' target range been copied instead, the result of the various summations would have been wrong.

Now complete the insertion of functions and formulae in the rest of the worksheet, noting that 'Total Costs' is the summation of rows 8 through 13, 'Profit' is the subtraction of 'Total Costs' from 'Consultancy', and that 'Cumulative' in row 19 refers to cumulative profit.

Then add another column to your worksheet to calculate (and place in column F) the average monthly values of earnings, costs, and profit, using the =AVG( ) function.

The worksheet, up to this point, should look like the one on the next page. To make room on the screen for all 6 columns, we changed the Font to Courier 10 points, but we could have used the **View**, **Zoom** feature instead. We also emboldened all the column and row titles.

PROJECT ANALYSIS: ADEPT CONSULTANTS LTD

Cell reference: F15 =AVG(B15:D15)

	Jan	Feb	Mar	1st Quart	Average
Consultancy	£14,000.00	£15,000.00	£16,000.00	£45,000.00	£15,000.00
Costs:					
Wages	£2,000.00	£3,000.00	£4,000.00	£9,000.00	£3,000.00
Travel	£400.00	£500.00	£600.00	£1,500.00	£500.00
Rent	£300.00	£300.00	£300.00	£900.00	£300.00
Heat/Light	£150.00	£200.00	£150.00	£500.00	£166.67
Phone/Fax	£250.00	£300.00	£350.00	£900.00	£300.00
Adverts	£1,100.00	£1,200.00	£1,300.00	£3,600.00	£1,200.00
Total Costs	£4,200.00	£5,500.00	£6,700.00	£16,400.00	£5,466.67
Profit	£9,800.00	£9,500.00	£9,300.00	£28,600.00	£9,533.33
Cumulative	£9,800.00	£19,300.00	£28,600.00		

Erasing Cell Contents:

If you make any mistakes and copy information into cells you did not mean to, then choose the **Edit, Clear** command. To blank the contents within a range of adjacent cells, first select the cell block, then use the command.

Once you are satisfied that what appears on your screen is the same as our example, use the **File Save As** command to save your worksheet under the filename **Project3**, as we shall be using this example in the next chapter.

Quick Key Combinations

We have already discussed how you can move around a worksheet, edit information in a cell, or mark a range of cells using the pull-down sub-menus, or the Toolbar.

Another method of achieving these and other operations (some of which will be discussed in the next chapter) is by the use of quick key combinations, which do not require the menu bar to be activated. As you get used to the Works package, you might find it easier to use some of the quick key combinations which can save you a lot of time.

The following key combinations are some of those for use with the spreadsheet tool.

Moving and Selecting

Go To	F5
Move right one window	Ctrl+PgDn
Move left one window	Ctrl+PgUp
Move to next named range	Shift+F5
Move to next unlocked cell	Tab
Move to previous unlocked cell	Shift+Tab
Select worksheet row	Ctrl+F8
Select worksheet column	Shift+F8
Select whole worksheet	Ctrl+Shift+F8
Activate Autosum	Ctrl+M

Editing

Copy contents of cell above	Ctrl+' (apostrophe)
Re-calculate now	F9
Open object menu	Shift+F10
Activate menu bar	F10

Working in the formula bar

Activate/clear the formula bar	Backspace, or Del
Confirm information in a cell	Enter
Confirm a range of cells	Ctrl+Enter
Edit cell in formula bar	F2

Printing a Worksheet

To print a worksheet, make sure that the printer you propose to use was defined when you first installed Works, as described in Chapter 3. Once a printer has been selected, Works will continue to print to that printer from all the tools.

To print a worksheet, choose the **File**, **Print** command, or use the <Ctrl+P> quick key combination, both of which open the dialogue box, shown on the next page. Clicking on the Print Toolbar icon will send to the printer without giving you a chance to check, or change, your settings, or what is sent.

Note that the default print settings are 1 copy, **All** pages, and all text styles, etc. You can change any of the options by choosing to print a different **Number of copies**, selecting which pages to print, and setting **Draft quality printing** output, if you wish.

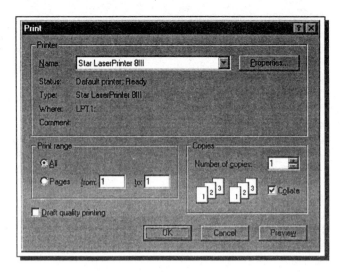

Before printing to paper, select the **File**, **Print Preview** command, or click the Print Preview Toolbar icon, shown here, to see how much of your worksheet will fit on your selected paper size. This depends very much on the chosen font. If the **Print Preview** option displays only part of your worksheet, and you then direct output to the printer, what does not fit on one page will be printed out on subsequent pages. To fit more of your worksheet on one page, you should reduce the selected font. Thus, the **Print Preview** option allows you to see the layout of the final printed page, which can save a few trees and, equally important to you, a lot of frustration and wear and tear on your printer.

Setting a Print Area:

To select a smaller print area than the current worksheet, first block the required area, then choose the **Format**, **Set Print Area** command and press **OK**. You can then either preview the selected area, or print it on paper.

To reset the print area to the entire worksheet, choose the **Edit**, **Select All** command, then **Format**, **Set Print Area** once more, before attempting to either preview your worksheet or send it to the printer.

Adding Headers and Footers

Headers and footers can be used in both the Works for Windows 95 Spreadsheet and Database tools. These cannot be viewed in the actual spreadsheets, but appear on the print output.

To add them choose **View**, **Headers and Footers** and type the required text in the **Header** or **Footer** boxes.

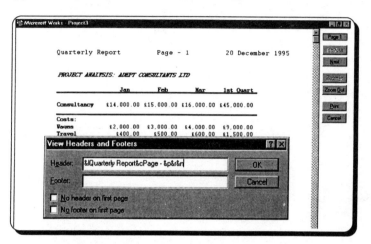

You can align parts of your headers or footers, and include other items automatically, by typing any of the special codes from the following list in with the text. Note that, unless you change the alignment, standard headers and footers are automatically centred.

Operation	*Special Code*
To align following text at left or right margin	&l or &r
To centre the following text	&c
To print page number	&p
To print filename	&f
To print date	&d
To print long date format	&n
To print time	&t
To print an ampersand	&&

As many of these codes as required, can be placed on a single header or footer line. Our example shows a line of **Header** codes entered and the resulting header in a print Preview of our example spreadsheet, **Project3**.

6. WORKSHEET SKILLS & GRAPHS

We will now use the worksheet saved under **Project3** (see previous chapter) to show how we can add to it, rearrange information in it and freeze titles in order to make entries easier, before going on to discuss some more advanced topics. If you haven't saved **Project3** on disc, it will be necessary for you to enter the information into the Works spreadsheet so that you can benefit from what is to be introduced in this chapter. Having done this, save your work before going on with the suggested alterations. If you have saved **Project3**, then choose **Existing Documents** from the Task Launcher and select the file from the list of recently used documents. On pressing **OK**, the worksheet is brought into the computer's memory and displayed on screen.

The Spreadsheet Toolbar

As with the word processor tool, mouse lovers have an advantage when using the spreadsheet, in that they can make use of the Toolbar, some of whose options we have already discussed. The Toolbar occupies the third line down of the screen. If you prefer, you can turn it off by activating the **View**, **Tool<u>b</u>ar** command. This is a toggle switch, when the '√' shows the Toolbar will display, otherwise it will not. The only advantage to be gained by not showing the Toolbar, is that you gain one line on your screen display.

To use the Toolbar you simply click the mouse on one of the icon buttons shown below, and the command selected will be effected on worksheet cells that are highlighted.

The meanings of the Toolbar options are as follows:

Option	*Result*
 Courier New	Choose a font from available list. Clicking the down arrow (↓) will open the list of fonts.
 8	Choose from available point sizes. Clicking the arrow (↓) will open the list of sizes.
	Open the Task Launcher
	Save current document
	Print current document
	Print preview
	Cut to clipboard
	Copy to clipboard
	Paste from clipboard
	Embolden selected text
	Make selected text italic
	Underline selected text
	Left align a paragraph

	Centre align a paragraph
	Right align a paragraph
	Autosum a column, or row
	Format selected cells as currency, with 2 decimal places
	Use Easy Calc to enter functions
	Create a chart using the selected entry data
	Create, or access, an address book

Controlling Cell Contents

We will now add some more information to the worksheet with the insertion of another quarter's figures between columns E and F. In fact, we need to insert four columns altogether.

In general, you can insert or delete columns and rows in a worksheet, copy cell contents (including formulae) from one part of the worksheet to another and freeze titles in order to make entries into cells easier.

Inserting Rows & Columns:

To insert columns into a worksheet, point to the column heading where a column is to be inserted, in our case F, and press the left mouse button, which highlights the whole column. Then choose the **Insert**, **Insert Column** command. Had you highlighted a specific cell, say F1, the **Insert** menu command would give you the options of inserting either columns, or rows.

Repeat the insertion command three more times so that the column headed 'Average' appears in column J. To insert three columns in one operation, select the three columns to the right of where you want the insertion before you choose the **Insert**, **Insert Column** command. We could now start entering information into the empty columns, but if we did this we would then have to re-enter all the formulae used to calculate the various results for the first quarter.

An alternative, much easier, way is to copy everything from the first quarter to the second and then only edit the actual numeric information within the various columns. We will choose this second method to achieve our goal. First, highlight the cell block B3:E19, move the highlighter to the top border of the block where it will change to a DRAG pointer. Hold down the <Ctrl> key and Drag copy the block four columns to the right, as shown below.

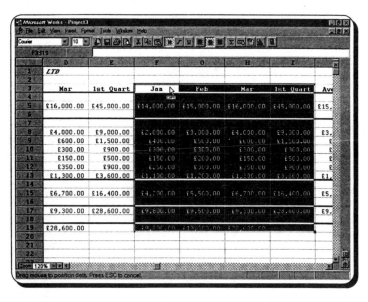

If necessary, use the **Format, Column Width** command, to change the width of any cells from 10 characters to 12. Now the widths of the highlighted columns are suitably adjusted, edit the copied headings 'Jan', 'Feb', 'Mar', and '1st Quart' to 'Apr', 'May', 'Jun', and '2nd Quart'. Save the resultant work under the filename **Project4** (don't forget to use the **Save As** command)!

Freezing Titles:

Note that by the time the highlighted bar is moved to column J, the 'titles' in column A have scrolled to the left and are outside the viewing area of the screen. This will make editing of numeric information very difficult if we can't see what refers to what. Therefore, before we attempt any further editing, it would be a good idea to use the 'Titles' command to freeze the titles in column A and rows 1 to 3.

To freeze column (or row) headings on a worksheet, move the highlighted bar to the cell below the column (or to the right of the row) you wish to freeze on the screen (in our case B4), and select the **Format**, **Freeze Titles** toggle command.

On execution, the headings on the chosen column (and row) are frozen but the highlighter can still be moved into the frozen area. Moving around the worksheet, leaves the headings in these columns (and/or rows) frozen on the screen. Carry this out and change the numbers in the worksheet cells F5 to H13 to those below.

Save the file again, but this time use the Save Toolbar icon, to keep the name **Project4**.

Note: If you examine this worksheet carefully, you will notice that two errors have occurred; one of these has to do with the average calculation in column J, while the other has to do with the accumulated values in the second quarter.

Non-Contiguous Address Range:

The calculations of average values in column J of the above worksheet are wrong because the range values in the formula are still those entered for the first quarter only.

To correct these, highlight cell J5 and press **F2** to edit the formula displayed in the formula bar from =AVG(B5:D5) to

```
=AVG(B5:D5,F5:H5)
```

which on pressing <Enter> changes the value shown in cell J5. Note the way the argument of the function is written when non-contiguous address ranges are involved. Here we have two such address ranges, B5:D5 and F5:H5, which we separate with a comma.

Now replicate the formula to the J8:J13 cell range by highlighting cell J5, choosing the **Edit, Copy** command, or <Ctrl+C>, move the highlight to cell J8 and use **Edit, Paste**. Then drag the highlight from J8 to J13 (to select the range) and choose the **Edit, Fill Down** command. Finally, repeat the **Paste** operation for the target cells J15 and J17.

You could also do all these actions with the Copy and Paste icons. The choice is yours!

Relative and Absolute Cell Addresses:

Entering a mathematical expression into Works, such as the formula in cell C19 which was

```
=B19+C17
```

causes Works to interpret it as 'add the contents of cell one column to the left of the current position, to the contents of cell two rows above the current position'. In this way, when the formula was later replicated into cell address D19, the contents of the cell relative to the left position of D19 (i.e. C19) and the contents of the cell two rows above it (i.e. D17) were used, instead of the original cell addresses entered in C19. This is relative addressing.

To see the effect of relative versus absolute addressing, type in cell E19 the formula

    =E5-E15

which will be interpreted as relative addressing. Now, add another row to your worksheet, namely 'Profit/Quart' in row 21, and copy the formula in cell E19 to cell E21, using the **Edit Copy** command. The displayed calculated value in E21 is, of course, wrong (negative) because the cell references in the copied formula are now given as

    =E7-E17

as the references were copied relatively.
   Now change the formula in E19 by editing it to

    =$E$5-$E$15

which is interpreted as absolute addressing. Copying this formula into cell E21 calculates the correct result. Highlight cell E21 and observe the cell references in its formula; they have not changed from those of cell E19.

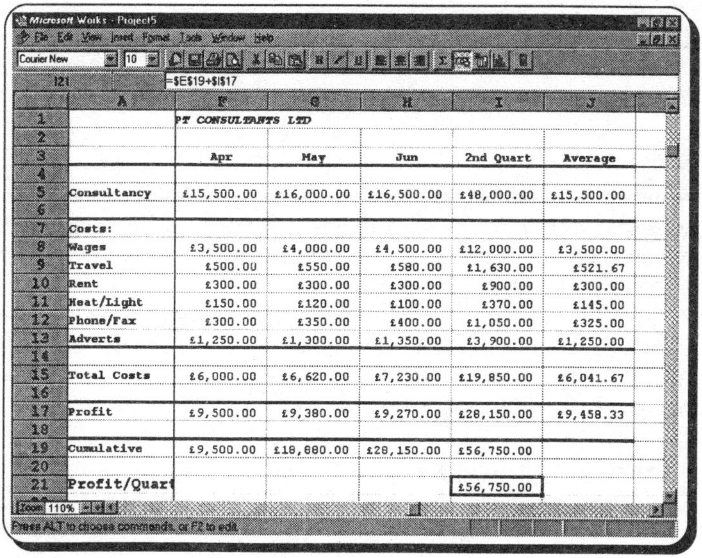

The $ sign must prefix both the column reference and the row reference. Mixed cell addressing is permitted; as for example when a column address reference is needed to be taken as absolute, while a row address reference is needed to be taken as relative. In such a case, only the column letter is prefixed by the $ sign.

Finally, correct the formulae in cells I19 and I21 (they should both contain '=$E$19+$I$17') in order to obtain the results shown on the previous page.

Moving Cell Contents:

To improve the printed output of **Project4**, we could move the caption to somewhere in the middle of the worksheet. Since the cell whose contents we propose to move is frozen, the move command has to be preceded by additional keystrokes. From the keyboard, first unfreeze the title with the **Format, Freeze Titles** command. Now, highlight cell A1 and choose the **Edit, Cut** command (or <Ctrl+X>), which removes the cell contents from the worksheet and places them on the Windows clipboard, then highlight cell F1 and **Paste** the clipboard's contents. Save the resultant worksheet under the filename **Project5**.

Other Useful Features

Works for Windows 95 includes several other spreadsheet features worth briefly mentioning.

Alignment:

Another method of carrying out the title formatting in the last example would be to use the ability to centre a cell's contents within a selected range with the **Format, Alignment, Center across selection** command.

Some other features to note in this dialogue box are the vertical alignment options and the ability to **Wrap text** (but not numbers or formulae) within a cell. You can now have several lines of text in the same cell.

Automatic Column Widths:

Choosing the **Best Fit** check box in the **Format, Column Width** dialogue box lets Works determine the best column width to accommodate all the entries in selected columns, or parts of columns. You could use this after selecting the whole sheet and not have to worry about cell widths again.

Inserting Functions:

You can automatically choose a function with the **Insert**, **Function** command and Works inserts it, including its arguments, into the formula bar. This feature saves you having to remember all the available function names, and from looking up the argument details every time. But remember they are all listed in the Appendix at the back of this book.

The UNDO Command:

The **Edit**, **Undo..** command reverses certain commands, or deletes the last entry you typed, but only if it is used straight away. Immediately after you undo an action, this command changes to **Redo..**, which allows you to reverse the action.

Automatic Cell Fill:

A useful feature which could save you much typing is the **Edit**, **Fill Series** command, which fills highlighted cells with a series of numbers or dates. You type the first entry, highlight the cells to fill and use this command to quickly enter the rest of a series of consecutive dates or numbers in the column or row.

Try typing 'Jan' in a heading cell, highlight the next eleven cells to the right, use the **Edit**, **Fill Series** command, select **Month**, and see what happens. Computers are supposed to make things easier after all!

Cell Formatting Options:

The **Format**, **Shading** command gives you control over the pattern and colour of the background of highlighted cells. To change the foreground colour of a cell's contents you must use the **Format**, **Font and Style**, **Color** option.

The **Format**, **AutoFormat** option gives a series of built-in formats you can apply to any highlighted range to give it a more 'professional' appearance.

Adding Spreadsheet Charts

Works 95 allows you to represent information in graphical form which makes data more accessible to non-expert users who might not be familiar with the spreadsheet format. In any case, the well known saying 'a picture is worth a thousand words', applies equally well to charts and figures.

You use the charting facility of Works by first selecting a data range to be charted on your worksheet, such as A8:D10 on our file **Project5**, and then choosing the **Tools**, **Create New Chart** command, or pressing the New Chart Toolbar icon. This opens the New Chart box, shown below. To see what types of chart, or graphs, are available click the icons in the **What type of chart do you want?** section. An example of each, based on the selected spreadsheet data, is shown in the box.

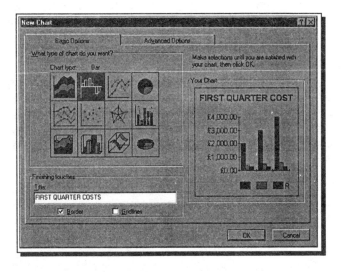

Although Works for Windows has eight main two-dimensional, and four three-dimensional, chart and graph types, there are many optional ways to view each type, and they can be grouped and overlapped, which allows you to add considerably to the list. All the different chart-types are selected from the box above, which is opened from the menu, or the Toolbar, when you are in a charting window.

To enhance your charts you can add titles, legends, labels, and can select grids, fill types, scaling, fonts, etc. These charts (you can have several per spreadsheet) can be displayed on the screen and can be sent to an appropriate output device, such as a plotter or printer.

The main graph types available are listed below, with their Charting Toolbar icons, where available. They are normally used for the following relationships between data:

Area

for comparing value changes to the total over a period of time; 2-D or 3-D options available.

Bar

for comparing differences in data over a period of time. Displays the values of dependent variables as vertical columns. The stacked and 100% options, show relationships to the whole; 2-D or 3-D options available.

Line

for representing data values with points joined by lines and appearing at equal intervals along the x-axis. For such charts, the x-axis could be intervals in time, such as labels representing months; 2-D or 3-D options available.

Pie

for comparing parts with the whole. Displays data blocks as slices of a pie. Can contain only one series; 2-D or 3-D options available.

Stacked Line

for representing the total in each category. A line chart in which the lines are stacked.

XY (Scatter)

for showing the relationship, or degree of relationship, between numeric values in different groups of data; used for finding patterns or trends in data (whether variables are dependent on or affect one another).

Radar   for showing changes in data relative to a centre point and to other data; useful for relative comparisons.

Combination   for displaying related data measured in different units; used for comparing two different kinds of data or to show a correlation that might be difficult to recognise.

Charts can be displayed on the screen at the same time as the worksheet, but in a separate window. As charts are dynamic, any changes made to the data are automatically reflected on the defined charts.

Preparing for a Bar Chart:

In order to illustrate some of the graphing capabilities of Works for Windows 95, we will now plot an income from consultancies graph of the **Project5** file.

First we need to define what we want to chart. The specified range of data to be charted should be contiguous for each chart. But, in our example, the range of data is split into two areas; Jan-Mar (occupying cell positions B3:D3), and Apr-Jun (occupying cell positions F3:H3), with the corresponding income values in cells B5:D5 and F5:H5. Thus, to create an appropriate contiguous data range, we must first replicate the labels and values of these two range areas in another area of the spreadsheet (say, beginning in cell B23 for the actual month labels and B24 for the values of the corresponding income), as shown on the next page.

To do this, use the **Edit, Copy** and **Paste** commands to copy the labels in the above two cell-ranges into the target area. However, before you replicate the cells containing numeric values, consider what might happen if these cells contain formulae, and you used the **Edit, Paste** command to replicate them. Using this command would cause the relative cell addresses to adjust to the new locations and each

100

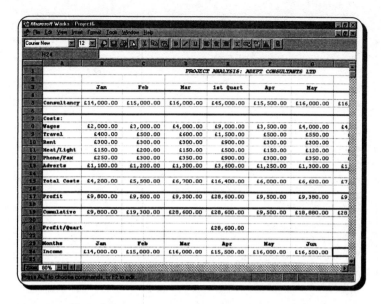

	Jan	Feb	Mar	1st Quart	Apr	May	
Consultancy	£14,000.00	£15,000.00	£16,000.00	£45,000.00	£15,500.00	£16,000.00	£16
Costs:							
Wages	£2,000.00	£3,000.00	£4,000.00	£9,000.00	£3,500.00	£4,000.00	£4
Travel	£400.00	£500.00	£600.00	£1,500.00	£500.00	£550.00	
Rent	£300.00	£300.00	£300.00	£900.00	£300.00	£300.00	
Heat/Light	£150.00	£200.00	£150.00	£500.00	£150.00	£120.00	
Phone/Fax	£250.00	£300.00	£350.00	£900.00	£300.00	£350.00	
Adverts	£1,100.00	£1,200.00	£1,300.00	£3,600.00	£1,250.00	£1,300.00	£1
Total Costs	£4,200.00	£5,500.00	£6,700.00	£16,400.00	£6,000.00	£6,620.00	£7
Profit	£9,800.00	£9,500.00	£9,300.00	£28,600.00	£9,500.00	£9,380.00	£9
Cumulative	£9,800.00	£19,300.00	£28,600.00	£28,600.00	£9,500.00	£18,880.00	£28
Profit/Quart				£28,600.00			
Months	Jan	Feb	Mar	Apr	May	Jun	
Income	£14,000.00	£15,000.00	£16,000.00	£15,500.00	£16,000.00	£16,500.00	

formula will then recalculate a new value for each cell which will give wrong results.

The Paste Special Command:

The **Edit, Paste Special** command allows you to copy only cell references without adjusting to the new location. To do this, mark the cell range to be copied (in this case B5:D5) and choose the **Edit, Copy** command, move the highlighter to cell B24 and press **Edit, Paste Special**, select the **Values only** option from the displayed dialogue box and press <Enter>, or select **OK**. Now repeat the same procedure for the values under Apr-Jun, but copy them into E24 to form a contiguous data range.

Finally, add labels for 'Months' and 'Income' in cells A23 and A24, respectively, as shown above, and save the resulting spreadsheet as **Project6**.

Note - The above way of copying cells is fine for our example where the data will not change. If you have data that changes, however, you would want your graphs to reflect these changes. This is easy to do, you set the graphing cells to 'mirror' the main sheet cells holding the variable data, by entering a formula consisting of a '+' sign followed by the cell address to be 'mirrored'. In our case, for example, cell B24 would contain the formula

+B5

It would then always show the contents of that cell.

The Chart Editor

To obtain a chart of 'Income' versus 'Months', block cell range A23:G24 and choose the **Tools**, **Create New Chart** command, or the New Chart Toolbar icon and type a **Title**, such as 'ADEPT MONTHLY INCOME'.

Select **OK** to accept the default Bar chart type and Works clears the screen and draws a bar chart of the information contained in the blocked range of cells. This places you in 'Charting' mode and in a separate window. A new set of menu commands and a new Toolbar are available, as shown below.

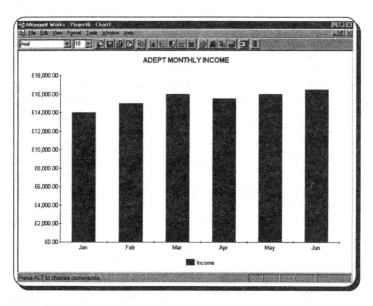

The chart is displayed in its own window, so to return to the worksheet you can press the <Ctrl+F6> keys, or use the **Window**, or **View** menu options. Choosing **View**, **Chart**,

102

reveals that the chart just displayed on screen has been given the name **Chart1** in the list box. To select a different type chart, you must return to Chart mode by selecting a Chart window. You can then choose the **F_ormat**, **_Chart Type** menu command to open the Chart Type box again, but with some extra options. You could select another type from the displayed list, but if you do your Bar chart will not be saved.

To select another type of chart, but still retain the first one, activate the **_Tools**, **Create _New Chart** command, which opens a new chart as **Chart2**. Choosing the Line option and selecting **OK** will produce a line chart similar to the one below.

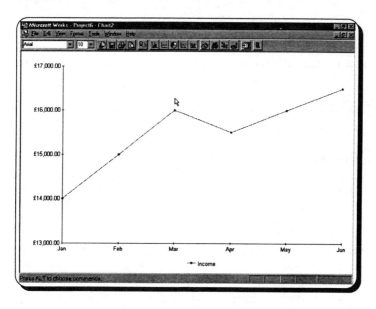

The shape of this line chart was improved by choosing the **F_ormat**, **_Vertical (Y) Axis** command and typing

```
13000
```

in the **_Minimum** box.

There are a lot of other options that you can specify when creating a chart. Some of these are self evident, like titles, legends, data labels, and the inclusion of axis labels and grid lines. These will be discussed only if needed in the examples that follow.

Saving Charts:

Charts are saved with a spreadsheet when you save the spreadsheet to disc. Thus, saving the spreadsheet under the filename **Project7**, will ensure that your charts are also saved under the same name. Since each chart is linked to the spreadsheet from which it was derived, if information on the spreadsheet changes, the charts associated with it will also change automatically.

Naming Charts:

You can give your charts more meaningful names than the default ones 'Chart1, Chart2 etc.' that are given by Works. The **Tools**, **Rename Chart** command opens a dialogue box from which you can select any of your charts and give them new names.

Customising a Chart

In order to customise a chart, you need to know how to add extra titles and labels, how to change text fonts, the colour and pattern of the chart, and how to incorporate grid lines.

Drawing a Multiple Bar Chart:

As an exercise, open **Project7**, if it is not already in memory, so we can build a new bar-type chart which deals with the monthly 'Costs' of Adept Consultants. As there are six different non-contiguous sets of costs, first copy them (including the cost description labels) using the **Edit, Paste Special** command, into a contiguous range below the 'Income' range (starting, say, at cell A27), as shown on the next page.

Having done this, copy the 'Months' labels from row 23 to row 26 and save the resultant worksheet under the filename **Project8**.

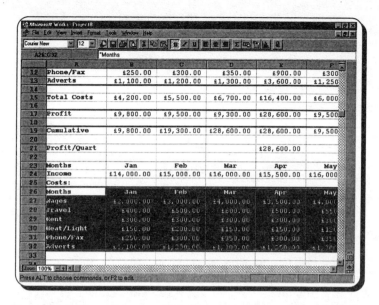

	A	B	C	D	E	F
12	Phone/Fax	£250.00	£300.00	£350.00	£900.00	£300
13	Adverts	£1,100.00	£1,200.00	£1,300.00	£3,600.00	£1,250
14						
15	Total Costs	£4,200.00	£5,500.00	£6,700.00	£16,400.00	£6,000
16						
17	Profit	£9,800.00	£9,500.00	£9,300.00	£28,600.00	£9,500
18						
19	Cumulative	£9,800.00	£19,300.00	£28,600.00	£28,600.00	£9,500
20						
21	Profit/Quart				£28,600.00	
22						
23	Months	Jan	Feb	Mar	Apr	May
24	Income	£14,000.00	£15,000.00	£16,000.00	£15,500.00	£16,000
25	Costs:					
26	Months	Jan	Feb	Mar	Apr	May
27	Wages	£2,000.00	£3,000.00	£4,000.00	£3,500.00	£4,000
28	Travel	£400.00	£500.00	£600.00	£500.00	£55
29	Rent	£300.00	£300.00	£300.00	£300.00	£30
30	Heat/Light	£150.00	£200.00	£150.00	£150.00	£12
31	Phone/Fax	£250.00	£300.00	£350.00	£300.00	£35
32	Adverts	£1,100.00	£1,200.00	£1,300.00	£1,250.00	£1,20
33						

Now block the cell range A26:G32, as shown, click the New Chart Toolbar icon, type 'ADEPT CONSULTANTS' in the **Title** field and press **OK**.

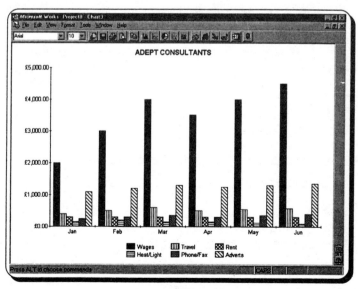

Immediately this is done, the bar chart of the 6 different monthly costs is drawn automatically with each month in a different colour. The diagram at the bottom of the previous page shows the result, after using the **View**, **Display as Printed** command.

Chart Titles, Fonts & Sizes:

To edit a chart title, choose the **Edit**, **Titles** command which causes this dialogue box to be displayed on your screen.

Type 'Monthly Costs' in the **Subtitle** field of the dialogue box and select **OK,** to complete the addition.

You can change the font and size of any contained text on a chart.

For example, click the title, to select it, and then choose **Format**, **Font and Style** to display the 'Font and Style - Title' dialogue box. From this you can choose any of the fonts available to Windows 95, or set a new size by selecting from the list of sizes (given in points), or change the colour and set other attributes.

To change the font of **all** the other text and numbers in a chart, choose **Format**, **Font and Style** without first selecting an item.

The fonts and sizes of the text in the chart on the facing page were set as follows:

Chart title: Bodini Book, bold and italic, size 16

Other text & numbers: Bodini Book, size 10

Grid lines were added by selecting the **Format**, **Vertical (Y) Axis** command and activating the **Show gridlines** option. We then saved the file as **Project9**.

106

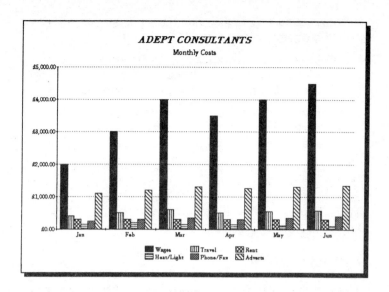

Printing a Chart:

Before printing, or previewing a chart, you should check your page settings with the **File**, **Page Setup** command. This opens the dialogue box shown below with the **Other Options** section active. You use these to control how a chart will be printed on the page.

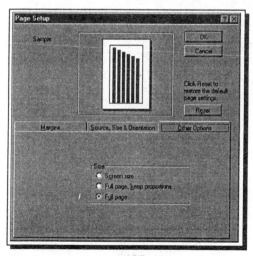

Screen size - prints the chart the same size as it appears on the screen - about a quarter page size.

Full page, keep proportions - prints charts so that they use the full paper width (between the margins), but scales the vertical size to keep the chart in proportion.

Full page - the default option, stretches the chart to take up the full page (between all four margins). This can produce some weird charts with portrait paper setting.

Before printing a chart it is wise to always Preview it, from the Toolbar icon. You may find that you have to adjust your text font settings to get all the chart text to display. When you are satisfied, press **Print** to record your chart on paper, or **Cancel**, to return to the chart window.

Drawing a Pie Chart:

As a second example in chart drawing, use the 'Average' values of the costs from the worksheet of **Project9** to plot a pie chart. Select the range J8:J13 and again, click the New Chart icon, select Pie as the chart type followed by **OK**.

Next, click the Pie icon on the Charting Toolbar followed by the **Variations** tab, and select the last of the six pie chart type options (in the bottom right hand corner) and press **OK**. Your range should now be displayed in a colourful pie chart.

The labels on each segment are not very self explanatory though. To remedy this, use the **Edit**, **Data labels** command,

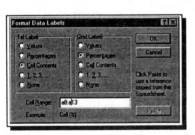

type A8:A13 in the **Cell Range** text box, as shown here, and select **OK** to leave the box and return to your chart.

Add an appropriate title to the chart and allocate a font and size to it as described previously.

Your chart should now look something like that shown on the next page.

To explode one of the segments of the pie chart, choose the **Format**, **Shading and Color** command and select the

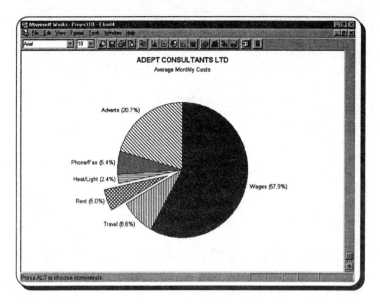

number of the slice you would like to appear detached, from the displayed dialogue box. Slices, in this case, are numbered from 1 to 6 and are allocated to the pie chart in a clockwise direction. Thus, to explode the 'Rent' slice, select **3** in the **Slices** box, then activate the **Explode slice** option and press the **Format** and **Close** buttons. In this way, you can emphasise one or more portions of the chart.

Finally, save the file as **Project 10**. Yes, with Windows 95 you can give all your files long names (up to 255 characters). You are no longer confined to the old MS.DOS 8.3 filenaming convention.

To cancel an 'exploded' selection, use the **Format, Patterns and Colors** command and press the **Format All** and **Close** buttons. Selecting other slices for exploding, without first cancelling previous selections, adds to the selection.

Mixing Chart Types:

To illustrate a combination of a bar and line chart, we will consider the variable monthly costs of Adept Consultants. This requires us to delete row 29 (the 'Rent' cost, which is fixed) from the worksheet. Just as well, since Works for Windows can only deal with a maximum of six categories and we would like to introduce average monthly costs as our sixth category.

Use the **Insert**, **Delete Row** command to delete the row dealing with 'Rent' from your worksheet, then create a new category in the renumbered row 32, to hold the average variable monthly costs. We will leave it to you to work out and place the cell formulae for this operation. If you have worked your way to here, this should not be too much of a problem.

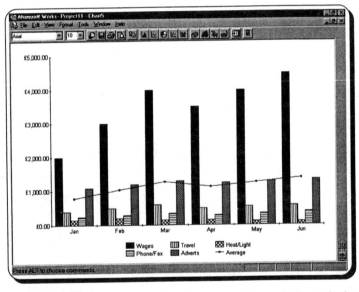

To create a mixed chart, like the one above, first mark the A26:G32 cell block and use the New Chart icon, select Combination and press **OK**. The chart may be a little mixed up, so use the **Format**, **Mixed Line and Bar** command, select the **Line L** option for the **6th Value Y-Series** from the revealed dialogue box, and **Bar** options for the other series, then press the **OK** button. Good luck.

110

7. THE DATABASE TOOL

A Works for Windows 95 database is a file which contains related information, such as 'Customers' Names', 'Consultancy Details', 'Invoice No.', etc. A phone book is a simple database, stored on paper. In Works, each record is entered as a worksheet row, with the fields of each record occupying corresponding columns.

The next section deals with the basic concepts of using a simple database, along with the database 'jargon' that is used in this book. If you are not familiar with database terminology then you should read this section first.

A database is a collection of data that exists, and is organised around a specific theme, or requirement. A database is used for storing information, so that it is quickly accessible. In the case of Works, data is stored in **data-files** which are specially structured files kept on disc like other disc-files. To make accessing the data easier, each row or **record** of data within a database is structured in the same fashion, i.e., each record will have the same number of columns, or **fields**.

We define a database and its various elements as follows:

Database	A collection of data organised for a specific theme.
Data-file	Disc-file in which data is stored.
Record	A row of information relating to a single entry and comprising one or more fields.
Field	A single column of information of the same type, such as people's names.
Form	A screen in which one record of data can be entered, displayed, or edited.
List	The whole database displayed in a spreadsheet-like format. Multiple records can be entered and edited.
Filter	A set of instructions to search the database for records with specific properties.

111

A good example of a database is a telephone directory. To cover the whole country many directories are needed, just as a database can comprise a number of data-files. The following shows how data is presented in such a directory.

```
Prowse H.B., 91 Cabot Close  ....................... Truro 76455
Pruce T.A., 15 Woodburn Road  ............... Plymouth 223248
Pryce C.W., 42 North Gate Road  .............. St Austell 851662
Pryor A., 38 Western Approach  ................ Plymouth 238742
Pryor B.E., 79 Trevithick Road  .................... Truro 742310
Queen S.R., 4 Ruskin Crescent  .............. Camborne 712212
```

Information is structured in fields which are identified below, for a single record, as follows:

Name	Address	Town	Tel No.
Pryor B.E.	79 Trevithick Road	Truro	742310

Creating a Database

A database file, in Works for Windows 95, is created either using a Wizard, or manually. Several very useful Wizards to help you rapidly design specific databases are provided with the package and are briefly described in Chapter 9.

Here, we are going to step you through the process of designing and building a simple database, suitable for keeping track of the invoices issued by a small engineering consulting company.

Selecting **Database from the Works Tools** section of the Task Launcher opens the screen shown on the next page, with its own menu and Toolbar (see end of Chapter), and the database file 'Unsaved Database 1' is opened as a default. You should not forget to change its name when you save it. All Works database files are automatically given the extension .WDB when they are saved.

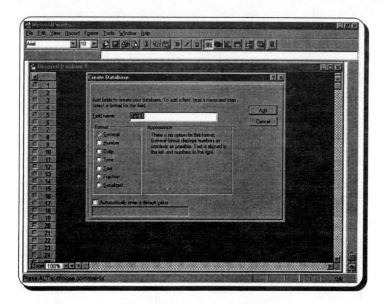

As shown, the Create Database dialogue box is opened automatically and is waiting for you to enter your database fields.

Entering Fields:

Type 'Customer Name' as Field 1 in the highlighted **Field name** text box and click the **Add** button to accept **General** as the format for the field data. The format determines how your data will be stored and displayed in your database. Clicking each format type in the list will show its description.

Enter the remaining fields as shown in the table below.

Field Name	Width	Format	
Details	20	**General**	
Inv.No	6	**Number**	(01235 - but 4 digits)
Issued	12	**Date**	(23/12/95)
Paid	10	**Number**	(True/False)
O/D	5	**Number**	(01235 - but 1 digit)
Total	10	**Number**	(£1,234.56 - 2 dec's)

The format examples shown above are those to select from the list of options given to you.

There are no more fields to enter so press **Done**. You should now have a basic, but empty, database in List View form which looks like the one shown below.

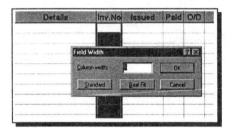

This List screen now has a row of field titles along the top, above an empty 'spreadsheet' working area. The default column width for a List screen is 20, and we want some of our fields to be shorter than that, so click the cursor in the title of the 'Inv.No' field, to select the column and choose the **Format, Field Width** command. Type **6** as the **Column width**, as shown here, and press **OK**.

Database Screens:

The opening screen of a Works 95 database is a 'List View' window, which gives a spreadsheet type view of the database, with the numbers down the left hand side referring to individual records, and the column headings referring to the database fields. The status line, at the bottom, shows which record the cursor is in, how many records are currently displayed, and how many are in the database.

The other way of looking at, and accessing, a Works database is through a 'Form' window, as shown next, which is a 'front end' to easily enter, and access, data. You use the **F9** key, or the Form View Toolbar icon shown, or the **View, Form** menu command, to change to the Form window.

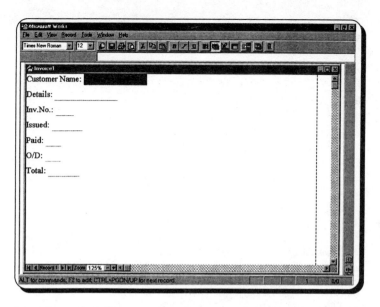

Pressing <Ctrl+F9>, or the Form Design Toolbar icon, or choosing **View, Form Design** will open a window in which you can customise the 'basic' form produced by Works.

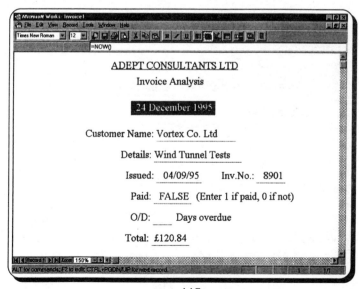

Pressing <Shift+F9>, or the List View Toolbar icon, or choosing **View, List,** will return you to the List screen.

Form Editing:

 Click the Form Design Toolbar icon, shown here, and use the Form Design window to alter the entry form for your database to something a little nearer ours at the bottom of the previous page.

As it is a multi-page window, the co-ordinate information on the line below the Toolbar could be needed to keep track of the current cursor position. This gives X and Y co-ordinates in the current system dimension units, (measured from the top left hand corner of each printed page). The page number of the current cursor position is shown on the Status Bar. The overall maximum form dimensions can be 3 pages long by 3 screens wide. A form can contain up to 256 database fields, as well as titles, labels and other text. Each field can hold up to 256 characters. A database can contain up to 32,000 records, which should be enough for most people!

Before entering any records, the entry form would benefit from some cosmetic attention. The List screen field widths are in fact independent of those of the Form screen. In our

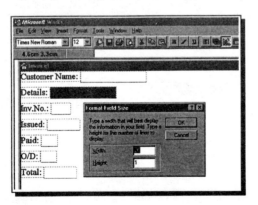 example, we want them to be the same, so place the cursor in the 'Details' field, click to select it and choose the **Format, Field Size** command. This opens the box shown, in which you can set the **Width** or **Height** of form fields. Accept **20** as the width and press **OK**. Then alter the other form widths to those given in the table on page 113.

When a field is selected in the Design window the mouse pointer changes and lets you drag an outline of the field around the screen. Move the fields so that all the colons are in one vertical line, or until you have a layout you prefer. With the Drag and Drop function you simply select a field with your mouse pointer and drag it to a new position.

To place a label on your form, click the cursor where you want it to start and type the label text. Type the database title

    ADEPT CONSULTANTS LTD

and drag it until you are happy with its position. Labels can be placed in any unused space on the form screen. With the title still highlighted it is a good time to carry out any enhancements. Click on the Underline Toolbar icon and then enter the other labels shown in our example (on page 115).

Hiding a Field Name:
The 'date' cell, shown in our example as 24 December 1995, is not a label. It actually has a dotted line below it and is, in fact, a database field (called Date:), containing a formula to generate the current date, but with its field name switched off.
    Place the cursor in position, and create a 'Date' field with the **Insert**, **Field** command. For the moment we will leave this cell empty. To hide it, highlight its field name, and choose the **Format, Show Field Name** command. The field name 'Date:' should now be turned off. If you wanted, you could now place a different label on top of it. This technique is useful if you want to keep actual field names short, but need longer descriptive ones on the front-end form, as could have been used with the 'O/D:' field (Overdue), shown in our example.

Entering Data in a Form
Now change to the Form view and enter the first record into the database. Your cursor should be in the date cell. Press <Tab> to move to the 'Customer Name:' field, and type the following:

Vortex Co. Ltd	press <Tab> and type,
Wind Tunnel Tests	press <Tab> and type,
4/9/95	press <Tab> and type,
8901	press <Tab> and type,
0	press <Tab> twice, and type,
120.84	press <Tab>

Nothing should have been entered in the 'O/D' field. The last <Tab> should have completed the entry of record 1, and brought up an empty form for the next record. Press <Ctrl+PgUp>, to move back one record, to the date cell of record 1.

When moving about a form, <Tab> and <Shift+Tab>, move the cursor between fields, whereas <Ctrl+PgUp> and <Ctrl+PgDn>, move between adjacent records.

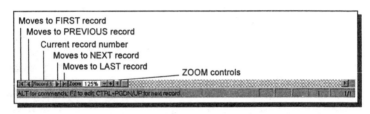

The arrow buttons on the left end of the Horizontal Scroll Bar can also be used to step through the records of a database, as is shown above.

Using Formulae in a Field:

Database formulae have two main applications; to automatically force the same entry in each similar field of every record in the database, or to calculate the contents of one field based on those of another. Each database field can only contain one formula. Once it is entered in the field of one record, it is automatically entered into all the other records. As in the spreadsheet, a formula is preceded by an equal sign (=).

In our database example we will enter formulae in two fields, the date formula next, and one that calculates the contents of a field, a little later on. Change to List view and with the cursor in the date cell, type:

=NOW ( )

As with the spreadsheet, this formula is shown on the screen, both in the cell and in the formula bar at the top of the screen.

When you press <Enter>, the cell may fill with the hash character (#). Do not panic, it only means the date is too long for the cell width. Simply alter the cell width with the **Format, Field Size** command, or re-size it with the pointer.

Protecting Fields:

You can 'lock' fields in your database to prevent their contents being accidentally changed, or to cause the <Tab> key to ignore the cell, when you are moving around the form, or entering data. To demonstrate this highlight the Date field in List View and use the **Format, Protection** command, click the **Protect field** option and press the **OK** button. The date field should now be fully protected. In fact, it is now inaccessible until the field's protection is toggled off again.

Now complete the data entry by typing in the remaining 14 records shown in the screen dump on the next page. In the 'Paid' field, enter 1 (TRUE) if the invoice has been paid, or 0 (FALSE) if not. When you have saved the database as **Invoice1**, a List view should then be similar to our printout.

Sorting a Database:

The records in our database are in the order in which they were entered, with the invoice numbers, in the 'Inv.No' field, shown in ascending order. However, once records have been entered, you might find it easier to browse through the database if it were sorted in a different way, say, in alphabetical order of 'Customer Name'. This might also make it easier to use the database for other operations, such as a mail merge. Works for Windows 95 has an easy to use sort

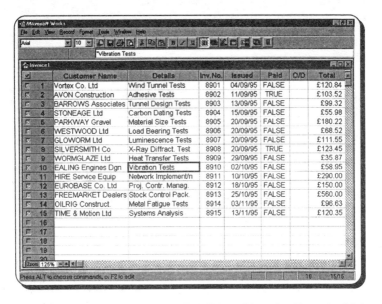

function, which can be accessed from either the Form or List screen.

With the cursor in any location, choose the **Record**, **Sort Records** command. Click the arrow in the **Sort by** drop-down list, select 'Customer Name', make sure **Ascending** is selected, and press **OK** to sort the database.

This sorts the field in an ascending order, from A - Z, and from 0 - 9. A descending sort order is the reverse. If you decide to have a secondary sort field (say you want invoices for the same company to appear in ascending order of invoice number), it is a simple matter to define a secondary sort range in the **Then by** box, before sorting. The three sort ranges available should be enough for most purposes.

Issuing these commands should produce the display shown on the facing page.

Now re-sort the database, in ascending order on the 'Inv.No' field, to return it to the original format.

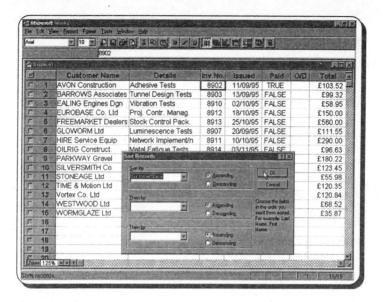

Date Arithmetic:

There are several date functions which can be used in Works for Windows 95 to carry out date calculations. For example, typing the function =DATE(95,12,24) - 24/12/95 backwards - works out the number of days between 31 December 1899 and that date. These functions are included to make Works more compatible with older versions of Lotus 1-2-3, but Works has an easier, and quicker, way of dealing with date arithmetic. Just typing a date into a cell, in one of the accepted date formats, allows Works to use the date number in any calculations. When a date is typed in a field, or a spreadsheet cell, what actually shows in that cell depends on the cell format. If '30/10/66', (a date in short date format), is typed into a cell, it will be shown as 30 October 1966 in long date format, or 24410, in any of the number formats.

The function

```
=NOW()-30/10/66
```

gives the difference in days (if the appropriate cell is formatted for integer numbers) between now and the mentioned date.

We will use this function to work out the number of overdue days for the unpaid invoices in our example, by typing the following formula into an O/D field cell in List View:

```
=NOW()-Issued
```

However, before we proceed any further, we should take into consideration the fact that, normally, such information would not be necessary if an invoice has already been paid. Therefore, we need to edit the formula to make the result conditional on non-payment of the issued invoice.

The IF Function:

The =IF function allows comparison between two values with the use of special 'logical' operators. The logical operators we can use are listed below.

Logical operators

=	Equal to
<	Less than
>	Greater than
<=	Less than or Equal to
>=	Greater than or Equal to
<>	Not Equal to

The general format of the IF function is as follows:

=IF(Comparison, Outcome-if-true, Outcome-if-false)

which contains three arguments separated by commas. The first argument is the logical comparison, the second is what should happen if the outcome of the logical comparison is 'true', while the third is what should happen if the outcome of the logical comparison is 'false'.

Thus, we can incorporate an =IF function in the formula we entered in the O/D cell, to calculate the days overdue, only if the invoice has not been paid, otherwise '0' should be written into that cell. The test will be on the contents of the corresponding 'Paid' field of a record, and will look for anything else but '0', or FALSE.

To edit the formula in the O/D cell, highlight any cell in that field and press the Edit key <F2>. Then press the <Home> cursor key, followed by →, to place the cursor after the '=' of the existing formula in the formula line at the top of the screen and insert

```
IF(Paid=0,
```

then press the <End> cursor key to move the cursor to the end of the existing entry and add

```
,0)
```

The edited formula should now correspond to that shown in the screen printout below.

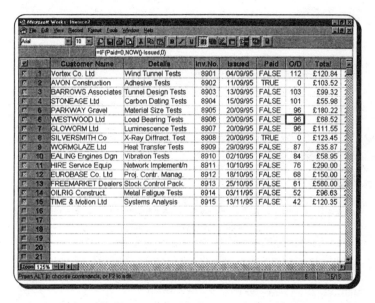

Note that once a formula is entered into any one field cell it is automatically copied to all the other cells in that field of the database. Save the file under the name **Invoice2**, but make sure you use the **Save As** command.

Your results will almost certainly differ from those above. The reason for this is, of course, that the NOW() function returns different numerical values when used on different dates. To get the same results as those shown, you could reset your computer clock to that used in our example. This is easily done from the Windows 95 Control Panel.

Save your work and Exit the Works program. Open the Control Panel (see page 77, if necessary), double-click the Date/Time icon, reset the **D**ate to '24/12/95' and press **OK**. Close the Control Panel and the new date will be operational when you re-enter Works for Windows 95.

WARNING - Make sure you have saved your work before doing this, and when you have finished this section remember to reset the date.

Searching a Database

A database can be searched for specific records, that meet several complex criteria, with the **T**ools, **F**ilters command, once a filter has been set as described below. Or, more simply, by clicking the Toolbar Filters icon, shown here. For a simple search, on one field only, the **E**dit, **F**ind command is, however, both quicker and easier.

We will use the previously saved database **Invoice2** to illustrate both these methods.

Let us assume we needed to find a record, from our database, containing the text 'x-ray'. In the List View window, choose **E**dit, **F**ind, type **x-ray** in the Fi**n**d what box, and select the option, **A**ll records. The record for 'SILVERSMITH Co' is brought to the screen, and the status line (1/15) indicates that this is the only record that meets the search criterion. Only the one record is shown, and all the others are hidden. The command, **R**ecord, Sh**o**w, **1** All Records will display the complete database again.

Database Filtering:

Sometimes it is necessary to find records in a database that satisfy a variety of conditions. For example, in a warehouse stock database, you may need to find all the items that were purchased between May and July of last year, that were ordered by a specific person, cost between £5.00 and £100.00, and that remained in stock for more than 60 days. In Works for Windows 95 this kind of search is called a filter.

When a filter operation is carried out in Works, all the records that match the filter criteria are extracted. In List View these are all displayed, whereas in Form view you see one matching record at a time. Every time a filter is applied the program searches the complete database for matches.

Retrieve the file **Invoice2**, if it is not already loaded, and select the List View. Clicking the Filters icon presents the Filter box, as shown below.

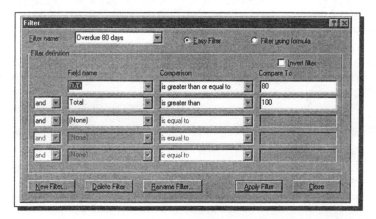

First type a name for the new filter if you want to. The above box is completed assuming that we would like to search the database for all the details of our customers whose invoices are overdue by 80 or more days, and who owe more than £100.

This intuitive approach to filters is very much easier than having to develop long logical expressions yourself. In fact what is actually created, in the above case, is the expression

```
='O/D'>=VALUE("80")#AND#Total>VALUE("100")
```

which is placed in the 'O/D' field cell of the filter.

When all the required criteria have been entered, select the **Apply Filter** button to action the filter. Unless you have renamed it, this first filter in your database will be **Filter1**.

You are then returned to List view, where only the records which meet the search requirements will be listed. In our case this should be three only. The screen should now look similar to that shown next.

✓		Customer Name	Details	Inv.No.	Issued	Paid	O/D	Total
☑	1	Vortex Co. Ltd	Wind Tunnel Tests	8901	04/09/95	FALSE	112	£120.84
☑	5	PARKWAY Gravel	Material Size Tests	8905	20/09/95	FALSE	96	£180.22
☑	7	GLOWORM Ltd	Luminescence Tests	8907	20/09/95	FALSE	96	£111.55
☐	16							
☐	17							

To view all the records again, choose **R**ecord, Sh**o**w, **1** All Records. The filter criteria will remain intact until next edited.

Marking Records:

You can now manually mark records that do not easily filter, by clicking in the box to the left of their row number, as can be seen above. Using the **R**ecord, Sh**o**w, **2** Marked Records will separate them for processing, or inclusion in a report.

The Database Toolbar

Most of the database Toolbar icons are common to the other Toolbars already described, but there are six icons on this bar specific to the database tool, whose meanings are as follows:

Option	*Result*
	Change to List view
	Change to Form view
	Change to Form Design view
	Change to Report view
	Insert new record
	Carry out a filter

8. DATABASE APPLICATIONS

Once a database has been created, the data sorted in the required order, and specific records have been searched for, the retrieved data can be browsed on the screen, either one record at a time, or in the list format, one full screen at a time. Some form of hard copy will almost certainly be required at some stage, by printing part, or all, of the database to paper.

Printing from a Database

There are three main ways of printing information from a database. In the 'Form' view, selected records are printed out in the same format as the screen form. Printing from a 'List' view will produce rows and columns just as they appear on the screen; little manipulation of the printed result is possible. To obtain a customised print-out, possibly containing selected fields only, but with report and page titles, totals and sub-totals, a 'Report' must first be defined. Data can then be printed from the Report screen. To see what will actually print use the Print Preview Toolbar icon.

What is printed from the List and Form windows is controlled by the settings in the **File**, **Page Setup**, **Other Options** dialogue box, as shown overleaf. Printing from List view, will produce a spreadsheet like layout, which will only be of use if your database has only a few fields per record.

Printing from the Form view could probably be best used with a diary type appointment database, or with a simple database designed to hold, say, personnel lists or parts inventories. Space could maybe be built into each form to hold a scanned photograph, for example.

To demonstrate the process, load the database **Invoice3**, which was created in the last chapter. From the Form view choose **File**, **Page Setup**, **Other Options** to display the dialogue box shown overleaf.

Switch off **Page breaks between records**, type '1' as the **Space between records**, and select **All items** as in our example. When you accept these settings a print preview should show two or three neatly spaced records on the page, depending on how you laid out your form, and what font size you chose.

127

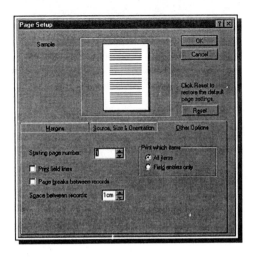

Creating a Report

A report can present records sorted and grouped, with summaries, totals, and with explanatory text. Once a report format has been set up, producing a report is a quick, almost automatic process. The current records 'displayed' in a database are those used to make the body of a report. The initial process is to create a report definition, which indicates what information will be in a report, and where it will be placed. Microsoft have given the Report facility of Works for Windows a 'semi-automatic front end' to make the production of simple report formats very much easier.

Using the database we built up in the last chapter, we will step through the process of setting up a report definition. If necessary, retrieve the file saved as **Invoice3**, which was a database to store details of the invoices sent out by a small company. It would be very useful, for both the accountant and the company management, if a report like that on the next page could be 'instantly' produced, and printed out. This summarises all the unpaid invoices and ranks them in groups depending on the number of months they have been overdue. Once we have defined the format of this report, it will only take a few keystrokes, at any time in the future, to produce a similar but updated report.

ADEPT CONSULTANTS LTD
Invoice Analysis Report

Summary of Overdue Invoices

Customer Name	Invoice Number	Days Overdue	Total Amount
TIME & Motion Ltd	8915	41	£120.35
OILRIG Construct.	8914	51	£96.63
1 - 2 Months Overdue	2	46	£216.98
FREEMARKET Dealers	8913	60	£560.00
EUROBASE Co. Ltd	8912	67	£150.00
HIRE Service Equip	8911	75	£290.00
EALING Engines Dgn	8910	83	£58.95
WORMGLAZE Ltd	8909	86	£35.87
2 - 3 Months Overdue	5	75	£1,094.82
PARKWAY Gravel	8905	95	£180.22
WESTWOOD Ltd	8906	95	£68.52
GLOWORM Ltd	8907	95	£111.55
STONEAGE Ltd	8904	100	£55.98
BARROWS Associates	8903	102	£99.32
Vortex Co. Ltd	8901	111	£120.84
3 - 4 Months Overdue	6	100	£636.43
Overall Totals and Averages	13	82	£1,948.23

Change to the Form Design screen of **Invoice3**, as we must first add an extra field to the form. This will show the number of months an invoice is overdue. We will need it, to provide the basis for sorting the database records, and breaking them up into groups.

Create a new field called 'Months' with the **Insert**, **Field** command, placed wherever you like on the form, but give it the integer **Number** format with **1** digit. Now change to Form View, highlight the empty cell, type the formula

```
=Int(O/D/30)
```

and press <Enter>. Note that Works places single inverted commas around the field name O/D, to show it as a label; this is because it contains the slash character '/'. The formula produces the integer part of the number of days overdue, divided by thirty. In other words, approximately the whole number of months overdue.

We are now ready to create the report definition. Choose the **Tools**, **ReportCreator** command, or click the Toolbar Report View icon. Ignore the initial Report Name box, but type ADEPT CONSULTANTS LTD into the **Report title** box of the main ReportCreator dialogue box, which is shown below.

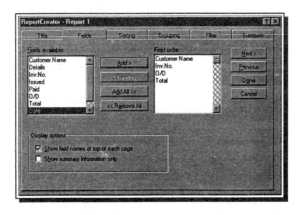

Click the **Next** button to move to the **Fields** tabbed section, select the field 'Customer Name' in the **Fields available** list box and press **Add>**, or <Alt+A>, to add the field to the **Field order** list. In the same way add the fields 'Inv.No', 'O/D' and 'Total' as shown above.

The other tabbed sections provide a quick way of entering instructions and formulae into the report definition, to carry out calculations and produce totals or averages, for example.

In the future you may find this an easier way to generate rapid reports, but at this stage we will not use this method, so press **Done** to move to the report definition screen, shown below.

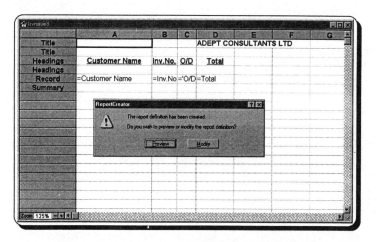

The message in the pop-up box suggests you use the Print Preview to see what your report will look like when printed, at this stage there is not much point, so select **Modify** which places you in Modify Report mode.

The working area of the screen contains columns and rows which intersect, as in the spreadsheet, to form cells.

The row types, shown on the left part of the screen, determine the order the rows will be printed in the report, and what action will be taken in that row.

Row type	Prints
Title	At the beginning of a report
Headings	At the top of each page
Intr *1st breakfield*	At the beginning of each group created by the 1st breakfield
Intr *2nd breakfield*	At the beginning of each group created by the 2nd breakfield
Intr *3rd breakfield*	At the beginning of each group created by the 3rd breakfield
Record	Each displayed record

131

Summ *3rd breakfield*	At the end of each group created by the 3rd breakfield
Summ *2nd breakfield*	At the end of each group created by the 2nd breakfield
Summ *1st breakfield*	At the end of each group created by the 1st breakfield
Summary	At the end of a report

At this stage the 'Intr' and 'Summ' line types do not appear on our screen, as there are no breakpoints defined for the report (more on this later!).

If you printed the report generated from this initial procedure we don't think you would be overly impressed with the results. As long as you can persevere, though, and follow us to the end of the chapter, we are sure you will be impressed with the power of the report generating facility.

Naming a Report:

If you open the **View** sub-menu you will see that a '√' has been placed against the **Report** option, which when selected opens a box showing the option **Report1.** Works for Windows 95 gives any reports generated a series of names, numbered 1, 2, 3, etc. To change this report name, choose **Tools**, **Rename Report**, type 'Overdue' in the text box and select **Rename** followed by **OK**. The **View**, **Report** box should now contain the option Overdue. When a database is saved, any report definitions generated are saved with it, including sorting instructions. Obtaining a similar report in the future is simply a matter of selecting it from the **View**, **Report** box.

Defining a Report:

The definition to automatically produce the report on page 131 is shown in the next screen dump example. This was designed to print on an A4 sheet of paper.

As an example we will step through the procedure of producing this report. Most of the reporting features should become apparent during the operation. You may also find it useful to spend a few minutes with the Works for Windows 95 Help sections.

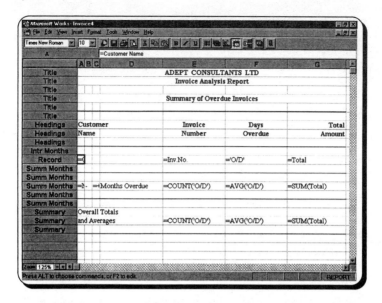

This report definition will be easier to prepare from an empty work area, so choose **Edit**, **Select All** and then **Edit, Clear** to clear the working area cells.

The first operation is to reset the column widths. Set columns A, B and C to a width of 2, by selecting these columns, choosing **Format, Column Width** and typing 2, followed by <Enter>. In the same way, alter the other columns as follows: D, E and F to 17 and G to 16.

Adding a Report Title:

The 'Title' rows hold any text that is to appear at the top of the first printed page of the report. In our example we will need six rows of this type, so we must insert four more. Press <Ctrl+Home> to move the cursor to the Home cell, highlight the top four rows by selecting their headers and choose **Insert**, **Insert Row**. The next box asks what type of rows are to be inserted; we want 'Title', which is highlighted, so press <Enter> to complete the operation

To position the main report title in the centre of the printed page, move the cursor to column A of the top row, type

ADEPT CONSULTANTS LTD

and press <Enter>. We will leave it to you to add the other two title lines in column A of rows 2 and 4. Now highlight the first four rows of columns A to G and use the **Format**, **Alignment**, **Center across selection** command.

To place the horizontal line across the page, select the cells A5 to G5 and place a **Bottom** line with the **Format**, **Border** command. There are several line options to choose from.

Adding Page Titles:

Page titles are placed in 'Headings' type rows, and appear below the report title on the first page of a report, and at the top of all subsequent pages. We will need three of this type of rows, so insert one more, as described earlier. The top two of these rows will hold the four report column titles, as shown on page 129. To enter these, place:

Customer and **Name**	- left aligned	-	in column A
Invoice and **Number**	- centre aligned	-	in column E
Days and **Overdue**	- centre aligned	-	in column F
Total and **Amount**	- right aligned	-	in column G

The way to select the above alignments is from the **Format**, **Alignment** box. Produce any lines with the **Format**, **Border** command, as described previously.

Using Formulae in a Cell:

The body of the report will be produced by the contents of the 'Record' row. If we type a field name, preceded by an equal sign, in a 'Record' cell, Works places the contents of that field for each record into the report.

There are also a series of statistical operators that can be included in cell formulae. These are mainly used in 'Summ' type rows, to produce totals, averages, etc. When placed in a 'Summ fieldname' row they give field statistics for the previous group printed. In a 'Summary' row the statistics refer to that field for the whole report.

Statistic	*Calculates*
SUM	Total of the group
AVG	Average of the group

134

COUNT	Number of items in the group
MAX	Largest number in the group
MIN	Smallest number in the group
STD	Standard deviation of the group
VAR	Variance of the group

There are several ways to enter formulae in a cell. If you can remember all your database fields, you could simply type the formulae in.

If not, the **Insert**, **Field Name** command places the selected field name in a cell, **Insert**, **Field Entry** places an '=' followed by the name; both dialogue boxes list all the fields of the database. The **Insert**, **Field Summary** box lists not only the database fields, but all the above functions, which you can select to place formulae in a 'Summ', or 'Summary', type row.

In our example, to complete the 'Record' row, enter the following formulae into the cells shown below and format the cells, in the **Format**, **Number** box as follows:

Cell	*Contents*	*Alignment*	*Format*
A	=Customer Name	Left justified	
E	=Inv.No.	Centre justified	Fixed (0)
F	=O/D	Centre justified	Fixed (0)
G	=Total	Right justified	Currency (2)

Sorting a Report:

A report is sorted to arrange the database entries in a certain order, such as alphabetical (order) or by date. A sort order specified in a report stays with that report, until it is physically changed. The main sort field, in our case, is on the Months field. We must specify the sort parameters now, as 'Summ' type rows cannot be used without a breakpoint having been entered.

The **Tools**, **Report Sorting** command opens the Report Settings dialogue box. The selections shown on the next page, are those required for our example. To obtain them, select 'Months' in the **Sort by** box and an **Ascending** sort.

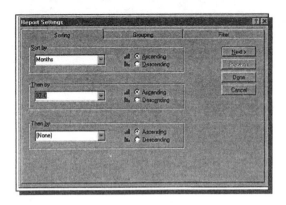

In our case, for neatness, we have also specified a **Then by** ascending sort on the 'O/D' field. If our database contained many hundreds of records, with several for each customer, we could also sort, and break, on the 'Customer Name' field. A summary for each customer would then be produced.

Click the **Grouping** tab and select the **When contents change** option, which will cause the report to split its output every time the value of the sorted field 'Months' changes.

Filtering a Report:

For a report to show the correct records, the database must first be searched using the required retrieval criteria, as was described in the previous chapter.

In our case, the report should include all the invoices which have not been settled. Click the **Filter** tab and choose **Create New Filter**, giving it the name 'Overdue'. Select the field 'Paid' in the **Field name** box, the statement 'is equal to' in **Comparison** and type '0' in the **Compare to** section and press **OK**.

When the above settings are accepted, two extra rows, 'Intr Months' and 'Summ Months', are placed in the report definition.

An 'Intr' row is placed before a report break section and can contain headings to identify the following data. In our case we will leave this line blank, or if you prefer you could delete it. It is only by 'playing around' like this and checking the printed results with Print Preview that you can fully master the report generator.

Completing the Report Definition:

Insert four more 'Summ Months' rows, and enter the following formulae in the middle row cells, with the formats and styles shown, as before.

Cell	Contents	Alignment	Format
A	=Months	Left justified	Fixed (0)
B	"–	Left justified	
C	=Months+1	Right justified	Fixed (0)
D	" Months Overdue	Left justified	
E	=COUNT('O/D')	Centre justified	Fixed (0)
F	=AVG('O/D')	Centre justified	Fixed (0)
G	=SUM(Total)	Left justified	Currency (2)

When you have completed this row, place horizontal lines, as described previously, above and below it.

Our report definition is almost complete now, only the 'Summary' rows remain to be done. If you have worked your way to this stage, entering these rows on your own should present no problems.

Insert two more 'Summary' type rows. Place a line in the bottom one, and type the following in the remaining two rows:

Cell	Contents	Alignment	Format
Row 17			
A	"Overall Totals	Left justified	
Row 18			
A	"and Averages	Left justified	
E	=COUNT(O/D)	Centre justified	Fixed (0)
F	=AVG(O/D)	Centre justified	Fixed (0)
G	=SUM(Total)	Right justified	Currency (2)

Printing a Report:

Printing a report is similar to printing a word processor document, except that the facility to force column page breaks is included, as is the case with spreadsheets. From the Report screen choose **File**, **Page Setup** and make sure your page is set up with a 3.2cm left margin, and select Print Preview to see what your report will look like on paper.

It should be similar to the screen dump shown below. Press **Print** to start printing, or **Cancel** to return to the Report definition screen.

ADEPT CONSULTANTS LTD
Invoice Analysis Report

Summary of Overdue Invoices

Customer Name	Invoice Number	Days Overdue	Total Amount
TIME & Motion Ltd	8915	41	£120.35
OILRIG Construct.	8914	51	£96.63
1 - 2 Months Overdue	2	46	£216.98
FREEMARKET Dealers	8913	60	£560.00
EUROBASE Co. Ltd	8912	67	£150.00
HIRE Service Equip	8911	75	£290.00
EALING Engines Dsn	8910	83	£58.95
WORMGLAZE Ltd	8909	86	£35.87
2 - 3 Months Overdue	5	75	£1,094.82
PARKWAY Gravel	8905	95	£180.22
WESTWOOD Ltd	8906	95	£68.52
GLOWORM Ltd	8907	95	£111.55
STONEAGE Ltd	8904	100	£55.98
BARROWS Associates	8903	102	£99.32
Vortex Co. Ltd	8901	111	£120.84
3 - 4 Months Overdue	6	100	£636.43
Overall Totals and Averages	13	82	£1,948.23

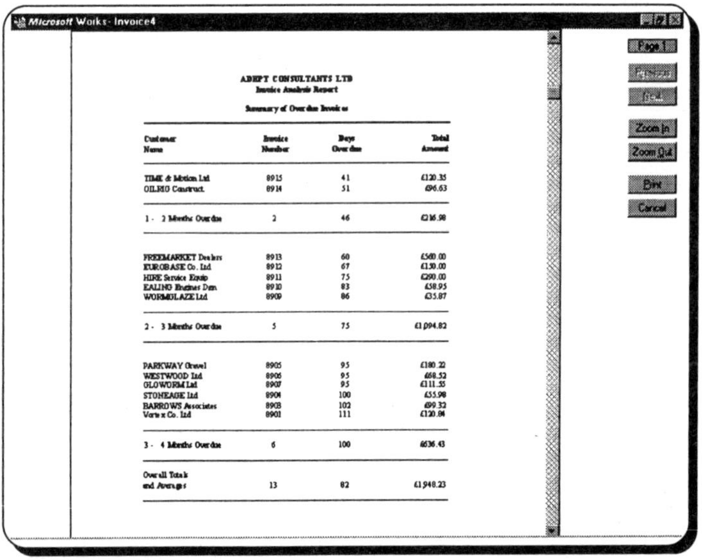

Our report definition is now complete. It probably took several hours to build, but an instant report can now be generated from it, no matter how big the database gets. Also you should by now be able to tackle any reports of your own design.

Form Letters

We are now in a position to use the mail merge capability of Works for Windows to create customised 'form letters', which make use of information stored in a database. As an example of this, you could create the simple database shown next, which contains the personal details of our potential customers. Save it as **Business Address**.

Now type the letter shown below it, using the word processor. Note the way the various field names are enclosed by angled brackets. These 'field name markers' cannot be just typed in place. Move the cursor to where you

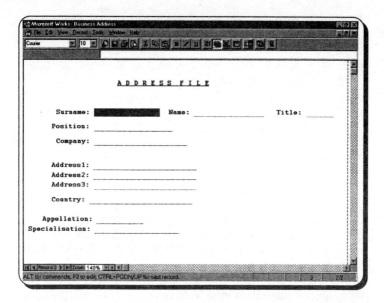

want a field name marker and choose the **Insert**, **Database Field** command. Click the **Use a different database** button and select the file name of the database to use, in our case

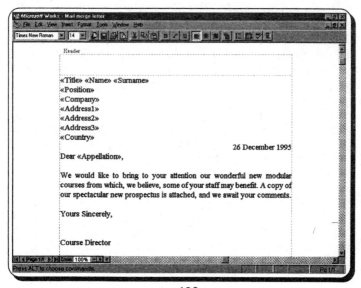

Business Address. In the **Select a field** box choose the field name you want, press **Insert** and then **Close** the box. Works will place the field name in the document. When the letter is completed save the document as **Mail merge letter**.

Note the field 'Appellation' which could be 'Sir', if you didn't know the name of the recipient, 'Mr Brown', if you did or 'John', if he was a friend of yours.

The field 'Specialisation' is included so that your form letters are only sent to relevant people. You would use information in this field in a Filter to select records.

Printing Form Letters:

Works for Windows 95 will print one copy of the letter for each record displayed in the database, assuming of course that you have entered some records. Before continuing make sure the database has been searched and sorted to display the records you need.

Open both the database file and the file holding the form letter. In our case **Business Address** and **Mail merge letter**. From the word processor file, make sure your printer is set up correctly, choose **File**, **Print**, make sure the option **Print Merge** is checked, click the **Preview** button and check what will be printed.

When you are ready, select **Print**, complete the usual Print dialogue box for **Number of copies**, etc., and finally press **OK** to start the print run. Obviously if you don't want to actually print the letters you would press **Cancel**.

That is all there is to it. As long as your printer does not run out of paper, Works will print as many letters as there are records selected.

This procedure is not, of course, restricted to producing letters. It can be used for any word processed document which extracts information from a database.

9. OTHER PROGRAM FEATURES

The Communications Tool

Works for Windows 95 includes a Communications tool that helps you to connect your computer to other distant computers, or to bulletin boards. This entails transferring information over a network, or over a telephone line with a modem.

When you open a new communications file by selecting **Communications** from the **Works Tools** section of the Task Launcher, the Easy Connect box helps you to enter the details of the service you want to contact, and then dials the connection for you. After your first session with a distant site, all your settings are saved when you save that Communications file. The next time you want to connect to it, just open the file in the Communications tool, and Works will make the connection for you.

We do not have space in this book to cover this aspect of Works, so only a mention is included. For more information about this, we suggest you use the **Help**, **Contents** command, click on the *Communications* icon and explore, as shown below.

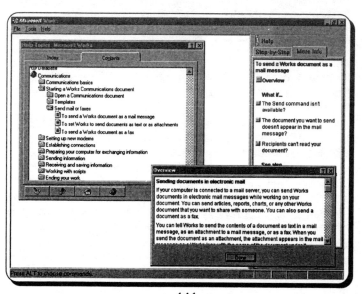

There are two more features included in the Works for Windows 95 package that need some coverage. These are TaskWizards and Templates, both of which are designed to make the program more useful and easier to use.

TaskWizards

With TaskWizards, re-named with this version of Works, you get step-by-step assistance in creating particular types of documents. There are 10 groups, set up for creating such applications as; address book databases, personalised letters, mailing labels, timesheets and many more. These

TaskWizards are produced by Microsoft and cannot be 'home made'; presumably they will continue to offer additions to the range in the future.

You start Task-Wizards from the Task Launcher, which is opened when you start the program, or use the **File New** menu command, or click the Task Launcher Toolbar icon, from any Works tool. All of these offer the above choice of TaskWizards.

If you are very new to Works 95, perhaps the **Start from scratch** Wizard in the Common Tasks section may be a useful place to start.

Also an Address Book is used by most people, and the Toolbars of all the Works tools include an icon to access such a database, so it would make sense to select the Address Book option next. Work your way through the initial screens, selecting what type of book to make and what extra fields and options to include, pressing the **Next** button to get to the next screen, whenever necessary.

When all the options required have been chosen, press the **Create It!** button, when it is offered, and sit back for a few minutes. Works goes into 'automatic mode' and with much flashing of screens builds up your database. In fact an in-built macro comes into operation, which is quite fun to watch.

The last screen, shown below, shows the Form view of a new and very professionally produced personal address book. You must agree that this is an easy way to create a new database, which offers quite a degree of customisation along the way.

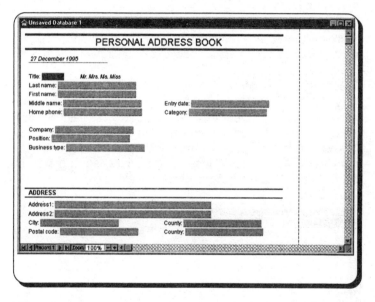

We strongly recommend you experiment with these automated procedures. They can often produce the results you want in a very short time. We have not spent much time explaining them, or covered them earlier in the book, for two very good reasons:

1.　They are very user friendly and almost anyone should be able to work through them without too many problems.

2. We feel strongly that you will become more proficient with the Works for Windows 95 program, as a whole, if you build your own applications.

Templates

A Template is a document 'blank' which can contain titles, text, formatting and other features, which do not change between documents of the same type. Once it has been created, you can open a Template, adapt the resulting open file in any way you want, without affecting the original template file.

Works 95 does not provide any templates for you, as most of those previously provided have now been incorporated into TaskWizards. You must now create your own.

Creating a Template:

A useful Template for almost everyone, would be a blank letter heading with your address, date etc., all laid out and ready to enter the letter contents. You could use one of the **Correspondence** TaskWizards to set up such a letter for the first time. Then to save time in the future, save the letter format as a Template before adding its text.

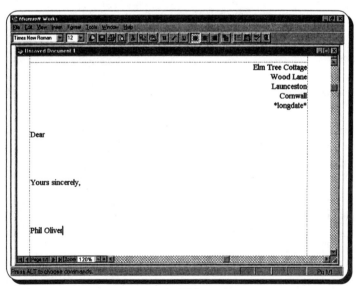

We prepared a simple fictitious letter heading, as shown on the previous page. It could, of course, have been far more sophisticated and included 'fancy fonts' and a graphic logo.

We suggest you do the same, and when you are happy with its layout and contents, choose the **File**, **Save As** command, click the **Template** button, type a suitable name, maybe 'Personal letterhead', and press **OK**.

In the future, whenever you want to send a letter, use your new Template instead of starting from scratch. To do this, go to the TaskWizards section of the Task Launcher, and you will find a new option - User Defined Templates - has been added to the bottom of the list.

Selecting this option and pressing **OK** will open a new document with all the text and formatting already included. All you have to do then is complete the body of your letter.

Many of the TaskWizards in Works 95 will produce output you could very usefully incorporate into your own Templates. We will leave it up to you to experiment with this.

Deleting and Re-naming Templates:

To delete, or re-name, Templates you have to use Windows 95 features. Templates are kept by Works in a folder called, 'Template', surprisingly enough. From within Works, use the **File**, **Open** menu command, click the 'Up One Level'

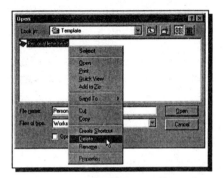

dialogue box Toolbar icon and double-click the Template icon. This will open the Template folder and should show you a list of all the Template files you have produced, in our case just the one.

Right-clicking on a file will open an object menu, as shown above. From this menu you can **Delete** or **Rename** the Template.

* * *

Works for Windows 95 has more commands and functions which can be used to build and run your applications and to link with other applications in special ways. What this book has tried to do is to introduce you to the overall subject and give you a solid foundation on which to build your future knowledge.

* * *

GENERAL GLOSSARY OF TERMS

Application
Software (program) designed to carry out certain activity, such as word processing.

Association
An identification of a filename extension to a program. This lets Windows open the program when its files are selected.

ASCII
A binary code representation of a character set. The name stands for 'American Standard Code for Information Interchange'.

Attributes
Indicate whether a file is read-only, hidden or system and if it has changed since the last backup.

Backup
To make a back-up copy of a file or a disc for safekeeping.

Base memory
The first 1MB of random access memory.

Batch file
An ASCII formatted file that contains MS-DOS commands which can be executed by the computer.

Baud
The unit of measurement used to describe data transmission speed. One baud is one bit per second.

BIOS
The Basic Input/Output System. It allows the core of the operating system to communicate with the hardware.

Bit	A binary digit; the smallest unit of information that can be stored, either as 1 or as 0.
Bitmap	A technique for managing the image displayed on a computer screen.
Boot	To start up the computer and load the operating system.
Booting up	The process of starting up the computer.
Browse	A button in some dialogue boxes that lets you view a list of files and folders before you make a selection.
Buffer	RAM memory allocated to store data being read from disc.
Byte	A grouping of binary digits (0 or 1) which represent information.
Cache	An area of memory reserved for data, which speeds up access to a disc.
Card	A removable printed-circuit board that is plugged into a computer expansion slot.
Cell	The intersection of a column and row in a spreadsheet, or database, which can hold an expression, a label or a number.
Check box	A small box in a dialogue box that can be selected (√), or cleared (empty).
Click	To quickly press and release a mouse button.

Client application	A Windows application that can accept linked, or embedded, objects.
Clipboard	A temporary storage area of memory, where text and graphics are stored with the cut and copy actions.
Close	To remove a dialogue box or window, or to exit a program.
Command	An instruction given to a computer to carry out a particular action.
Command line	The line in an MS-DOS window, or screen, into which you enter DOS commands.
Command Prompt	The prompt (e.g. C>) which appears on the command line to let you know that MS-DOS is ready to receive a command.
Computer name	The name that identifies a specific computer to other users of a network
Conventional Memory	The first 640KB of base memory.
CPU	The Central Processing Unit; the main chip that executes all instructions entered into a computer.
Cursor	The blinking line indicating where the next input can be entered.
Database	A structured file containing related information, or data.
DDE	Dynamic data exchange - a process that enables you to

	exchange data between two or more Windows programs.
Default	The command, device or option automatically chosen by the system.
Desktop	The Windows screen working background, on which you place icons, folders, etc.
Device driver	A special file that must be loaded into memory for Windows to be able to address a specific procedure or hardware device.
Device name	A logical name used by DOS to identify a device, such as LPT1 or COM1 for the parallel or serial printer.
Dialogue box	A window displayed on the screen to allow the user to enter information.
Dimmed	Unavailable menu options shown in a different colour.
Disc	A device on which you can store programs and data.
Disc file	A collection of program code, or data, that is stored under a given name on a disc.
Disconnect	To detach a drive, port or computer from a shared device.
Document	A file produced by an application program.
Domain	A group of devices, servers and computers on a network.
DOS	Disc Operating System. A collection of small specialised

	programs that allow interaction between user and computer.
DOS prompt	The prompt displayed in an MS-DOS window, or screen, such as A> or C>, indicating that DOS is ready to accept commands.
Double-click	To quickly press and release a mouse button twice.
DPI	Dots Per Inch - a resolution standard for laser printers.
Drag	To press and hold down the left mouse button while moving the mouse, to move an object on the screen.
Drive name	The letter (followed by a colon) which identifies a floppy or hard disc drive.
Driver	A set of commands used to run a peripheral device (see device driver).
EISA	Extended Industry Standard Architecture, for construction of PCs with the Intel 32-bit microprocessor.
Embedded object	Information in a document that is 'copied' from its source application. Selecting the object opens the creating application from within the document.
EMM	Expanded Memory Manager.
Enter key	The key that is pressed after entering data on the command line.

151

Expanded memory	This is memory outside the conventional RAM (first 640-KB) and is used by some MS-DOS software to store data and run applications.
Extended memory	This is memory above the 1-MByte memory address, all of which is used by Windows 95.
External command	A native command Windows executes by first loading it from a file.
FAT	The File Allocation Table. An area on disc where information is kept on which part of the disc the file is to be found.
File	The name given to an area on disc containing a program or data.
File extension	The optional three-letter suffix following the period in a filename. Windows 95 uses the extension to identify the filetype.
File list	A list of filenames contained in the active directory.
Filename	The name given to a file. In Windows 95 this can be up to 255 characters long.
Filespec	File specification made up of drive, path and filename.
Fixed disc	The hard disc of a computer.
Floppy disc	A removable disc on which information can be stored magnetically. There are two main types of floppy discs; a 5¼"

	flexible disc and a 3½" stiff disc.
Folder	An area on disc where information relating to a group of files is kept.
Font	A graphic design representing a set of characters, numbers and symbols.
Formatting	The process of preparing a disc so that it can store information.
Full screen	Used when an MS-DOS application takes up all the monitor screen.
Function	A built-in formula which performs specific calculations in a spreadsheet or database cell.
Function key	One of the series of 10 or 12 keys marked with the letter F and a numeral, used for specific operations.
Graphics card	A device that controls the display on the monitor and other allied functions.
GUI	A Graphic User Interface, such as Windows 95, which uses visual displays to eliminate the need for typing commands.
Hardcopy	Output on paper.
Hard disc	A device built into the computer for holding programs and data. It is sometimes referred to as a fixed disc.

Hardware	The equipment that makes up a computer system, excluding the programs or software.
Help	A Windows system that gives you instructions and additional information.
Highlight	The change to a reverse-video appearance when a menu item or area of text is selected.
HMA	High Memory Area; the first 64KB of memory beyond the end of the base memory.
Icon	A small graphic image that represents a function or object. Clicking on an icon produces an action.
Insertion point	A flashing bar that shows where typed text will be entered into a document.
Internal command	One of a set of system commands loaded into memory every time you start your PC.
Interface	A device that allows you to connect a computer to its peripherals.
IRQ	Interrupt request lines - hardware lines used by devices to signal the processor that they are ready to send, or receive, data.
ISA	Industry Standard Architecture; a standard for internal connections in PCs.
Key combination	When two or more keys are pressed simultaneously, such as <Ctrl+Esc>.

Kilobyte	(KB); 1024 bytes of information or storage space.
LAN	Local Area Network; PCs, workstations or minis sharing files and peripherals within the same site.
LCD	Liquid Crystal Display.
Linked object	A placeholder for an object inserted into a destination document.
Local	A resource that is located on your computer, not linked to it over a network.
Log on	To gain access to a network.
Long filename	In Windows 95 the name given to a file can be up to 255 characters long.
MCA	Micro Channel Architecture; IBM's standard for construction of PCs introduced in the 1990s.
MCI	Media Control Interface - a standard for files and multimedia devices.
Megabyte	(MB); 1024 kilobytes of information or storage space.
Megahertz	(MHz); Speed of processor in millions of cycles per second.
Memory	Part of computer consisting of storage elements organised into addressable locations that can hold data and instructions.
Menu	A list of available options in an application.

Menu bar	The horizontal bar that lists the names of menus.
Microprocessor	The calculating chip within a computer.
MIDI	Musical Instrument Digital Interface - enables devices to transmit and receive sound and music messages.
MIPS	Million Instructions Per Second; measures speed of a system.
Monitor	The display device connected to your PC.
Mouse	A device used to manipulate a pointer around your display and activate a certain process by pressing a button.
MS-DOS	Microsoft's implementation of the Disc Operating System for compatible PCs.
Multi-tasking	Performing more than one operation at the same time.
Network server	Central computer which stores files for several linked computers.
Operating System	A group of programs that translates your commands to the computer.
Password	A unique character string used to gain access to a network, or an application document.
PATH	The location of a file in the directory tree.
PCX	A standard file format used for bitmapped graphics.

Peripheral	Any device attached to a PC.
PIF file	Program information file - gives information to Windows about an MS-DOS application.
Pixel	A picture element on screen; the smallest element that can be independently assigned colour and intensity.
Port	An input/output address through which your PC interacts with external devices.
Print queue	The list of print jobs waiting to be sent to a printer.
Program	A set of instructions which cause the computer to perform certain tasks.
Prompt	The MS-DOS prompt displayed on the command line, such as A> or C>, indicating that DOS is ready to accept commands.
Protected mode	The operating mode of 386 (and higher) processors, which allows more than 1MB of memory to be addressed.
Protocol	Defines the way in which data is transferred over a network.
Processor	The electronic device which performs calculations.
PS/2	The range of PCs first introduced by IBM in the late 1980s.
RAM	Random Access Memory. The micro's volatile memory. Data held in it is lost when power is switched off.

Real mode	MS-DOS mode, typically used to run programs, such as MS-DOS games, that will not run under Windows.
Resource	A directory, or printer, that can be shared over a network.
ROM	Read Only Memory. A PC's non-volatile memory. Data is written into this memory at manufacture and is not affected by power loss.
Screen saver	A display program that moves images on an inactive screen, to prevent it burning out.
Scroll bar	A bar that appears at the right side or bottom edge of a window.
Sector	Disc space, normally 512 bytes long.
Serial interface	An interface that transfers data as individual bits; each operation has to be completed before the next starts.
Server	A networked computer that is used to share resources.
Shared resource	Any device, program or file that is available to network users.
Software	The programs and instructions that control your PC.
Spooler	Software which handles transfer of information to a store where it will be used by a peripheral device.

Spreadsheet	An electronic page made of a matrix of rows and columns.
SVGA	Super Video Graphics Array; it has all the VGA modes but with 256 colours.
Swap file	An area of your hard disc used to store temporary operating files, known as virtual memory.
System disc	A disc containing files to enable MS-DOS to start up.
Task Launcher	Opening dialogue box giving access to TaskWizards, existing files or the Works tools.
TaskWizard	An automated procedure to create a specific type of document.
Template	A file blank you can create to contain common text and formatting to use as a basis for new documents.
Text file	An unformatted file of text characters saved in ASCII format.
Tool	Works for Windows internal application, such as the word processor or spreadsheet.
Toolbar	A bar containing icons giving quick access to commands.
Toggle	To turn an action on and off with the same switch.
TrueType fonts	Fonts that can be scaled to any size and print as they show on the screen.
UMB	A block of upper memory made available by a 386 memory manager into which memory

159

	resident software can be loaded.
Upper memory	The 384KB of memory between the top of conventional memory and the end of the base memory.
VGA	Video Graphics Array; has all modes of EGA, but with 16 colours.
Virtual machine	A logical computer that Windows creates in memory.
Virtual memory	See swap file.
Volume label	An identifying label written to a disc when a disc is first formatted.
Wildcard character	A character that can be included in a filename to indicate any other character (?) or group of characters (*).
Windows 95	The graphical operating system under which this version of Microsoft Works is installed.
Word processor	One of the Works tools on which you create text and graphics based documents.

APPENDIX - FUNCTIONS

Microsoft Work's =functions are built-in formulae that perform specialised calculations in both spreadsheets and databases. Their general format is:

=name(arg1,arg2,...)

where 'name' is the function name, and 'arg1', 'arg2', etc., are the arguments required for the evaluation of the function. Arguments must appear in a parenthesised list as shown above and their exact number depends on the function being used. However, there are seven functions that do not require arguments and are used with empty parentheses. These are: =ERR( ), =FALSE( ), =NA( ), =NOW( ), =PI( ), =RAND( ) and =TRUE( ).

There are three types of arguments used with =functions: numeric values, range values and text strings, the type used being dependent on the type of function. Numeric value arguments can be entered either directly as numbers, as a cell address, a cell range name or as a formula. Range value arguments can be entered either as a range address or a range name.

In the spreadsheet tool you can automatically choose a function with the **Insert**, **Function** command and Works inserts it, including its arguments, into the formula bar.

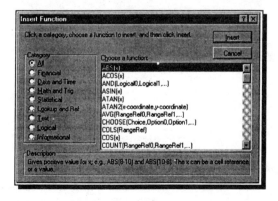

Types of Functions

There are several types of functions, such as mathematical, logical, financial, statistical, date and time, text, reference and informational. Each type requires its own number and type of arguments. These are listed below under the various function categories.

Mathematical Functions:

Mathematical functions evaluate a result using numeric arguments. The various functions and their meaning are as follows:

Function	Description
=ABS(X)	Returns the absolute value of X
=ACOS(X)	Returns the angle in radians, whose cosine is X (arc cos of X)
=ASIN(X)	Returns the angle in radians, whose sine is X (arc sin of X)
=ATAN(X)	Returns the angle (radians), between $\pi/2$ and $-\pi/2$, whose tangent is X (arc tan of X – 2 quadrant)
=ATAN2(X,Y)	Returns the angle (radians), between π and $-\pi$ whose tangent is Y/X (arc tan of Y/X – 4 quadrant)
=COS(X)	Returns the cosine of angle X, (X must be in radians)
=EXP(X)	Raises e to the power of X
=INT(X)	Returns the integer part of X
=LN(X)	Returns the natural logarithm (base e) of X
=LOG(X)	Returns the logarithm (base 10) of X
=MOD(X,Y)	Returns the remainder of X/Y
=PI( )	Returns the value of π (3.141593)
=RAND( )	Returns a random number between 0 and 1, excluding 1
=ROUND(X,N)	Returns the value of X rounded to N places

=SIN(X)	Returns the sine of angle X (X must be in radians)
=SQRT(X)	Returns the square root of X
=TAN(X)	Returns the tangent of angle X (X must be in radians).

Logical Functions:

Logical functions produce a value based on the result of a conditional statement, using numeric arguments. The various functions and their meanings are as follows:

Function	*Description*
=AND(Ag0,Ag1...)	Returns 1 (TRUE) if all of the arguments are true, else returns 0 (FALSE)
=FALSE( )	Returns the logical value 0
=IF(Cr,X,Y)	Returns the value X if Cr is TRUE and Y if Cr is FALSE
=NOT(Ag)	Returns the opposite of logical value Ag
=OR(Ag0,Ag1...)	Returns 1 (TRUE) if any of the arguments are true, else returns 0 (FALSE)
=TRUE( )	Returns the logical value 1.

Financial Functions:

Financial functions evaluate loans, annuities, and cash flows over a period of time, using numeric arguments. The various functions and their meaning are as follows:

Function	*Description*
=CTERM(Rt,Fv,Pv)	Returns the number of compounding periods for an investment of present value Pv, to grow to a future value Fv, at a fixed interest rate Rt
=DDB(Ct,Sg,Lf,Pd)	Returns the double-declining depreciation allowance of an asset, given the original cost Ct, predicted salvage value Sg, the

	life Lf of the asset, and the period Pd
=FV(Pt,Rt,Tm)	Returns the future value of a series of equal payments, each of equal amount Pt, earning a periodic interest rate Rt, over a number of payment periods in term Tm
=IRR(Gs,Rg)	Returns the internal rate of return of the series of cash flows in a range Rg, based on the approximate percentage guess Gs of the IRR
=NPV(Rt,Rg)	Returns the present value of the series of future cash flows in range Rg, discounted at a periodic interest rate Rt
=PMT(Pl,Rt,Tm)	Returns the amount of the periodic payment needed to pay off the principal Pl, at a periodic interest rate Rt, over the number of payment periods in term Tm
=PV(Pt,Rt,Tm)	Returns the present value of a series of equal payments, each of equal amount Pt, discounted at a periodic interest rate Rt, over a number of payment periods in term Tm
=RATE(Fv,Pv,Tm)	Returns the periodic interest rate necessary for a present value Pv to grow to a future value Fv, over the number of compounding periods in term Tm
=SLN(Ct,Sg,Lf)	Returns the straight-line depreciation allowance of an asset for one period, given the original cost Ct, predicted salvage value Sg, and the life Lf of the asset

=SYD(Ct,Sg,Lf,Pd)	Returns the sum-of-the-years' digits depreciation allowance of an asset, given the original cost Ct, predicted salvage value Sg, the life Lf of the asset, and the period Pd
=TERM(Pt,Rt,Fv)	Returns the number of payment periods of an investment, given the amount of each payment Pt, the periodic interest rate Rt, and the future value of the investment Fv.

Statistical Functions:

Statistical functions evaluate lists of values using numeric arguments or cell ranges. The various functions and their meaning are as follows:

Function	*Description*
=AVG(Rg0,Rg1,...)	Returns the average of values in range(s) Rg0, Rg1, ...
=COUNT(Rg0,Rg1,...)	Returns the number of non-blank entries in range(s) Rg0, Rg1, ...
=MAX(Rg0,Rg1,...)	Returns the maximum value in range(s) Rg0, Rg1, ...
=MIN(Rg0,Rg1,...)	Returns the minimum value in range(s) Rg0, Rg1, ...
=STD(Rg0,Rg1,...)	Returns the standard deviation of values in range(s) Rg0, Rg1, ...
=SUM(Rg0,Rg1,...)	Returns the sum of values in range(s) Rg0, Rg1, ...
=VAR(Rg0,Rg1,...)	Returns the variance of values in range(s) Rg0, Rg1, ...

Text Functions:

Text functions operate on strings and produce numeric or string values dependent on the function.

Function	*Description*
=EXACT(Sg1,Sg2)	Returns 1 (TRUE) if strings Sg1 and Sg2 are exactly alike, otherwise 0 (FALSE)
=FIND(Ss,Sg,Sn)	Returns position at which the first occurrence of search string Ss begins in string Sg, starting the search from search number Sn
=LEFT(Sg,N)	Returns the first (leftmost) N characters in string Sg
=LENGTH(Sg)	Returns the number of characters in string Sg
=LOWER(Sg)	Converts all the letters in string Sg to lowercase
=MID(Sg,Sn,N)	Returns N characters from string Sg beginning with the character at Sn
=N(Rg)	Returns the numeric value in the upper left corner cell in range Rg
=PROPER(Sg)	Converts all words in string Sg to first letter in uppercase and the rest in lowercase
=REPEAT(Sg,N)	Returns string Sg N times. Unlike the repeating character (\), the output is not limited by the column width
=REPLACE(O,S,N,Ns)	Removes N characters from original string O, starting at character S and then inserts new string Ns in the vacated place
=RIGHT(Sg,N)	Returns the last (rightmost) N characters in string Sg
=S(Rg)	Returns the string value in the upper left corner cell in range Rg
=STRING(X,N)	Returns the numeric value X as a string, with N decimal places

=TRIM(Sg)	Returns string Sg with no leading, trailing or consecutive spaces
=UPPER(Sg)	Converts all letters in string Sg to uppercase
=VALUE(Sg)	Returns the numeric value of string Sg.

Date and Time Functions:

Date and time functions generate and use serial numbers to represent dates and times. Each date between 1 January, 1900 and 31 December 2079 has an integer serial number starting with 1 and ending with 65534. Each moment during a day has a decimal serial number starting with 0.000 at midnight and ending with 0.99999 just before the following midnight. Thus the value 0.5 indicates midday. The various functions and their meanings are as follows:

Function	*Description*
=DATE(Yr,Mh,Dy)	Returns the date number of Yr,Mh,Dy
=DAY(Dn)	Returns the day number of date number Dn
=HOUR(Tn)	Returns the hour number of time number Tn
=MINUTE(Tn)	Returns the minute number of time number Tn
=MONTH(Dn)	Returns the month number of date number Dn
=NOW( )	Returns the serial number for the current date and time
=SECOND(Tn)	Returns the second number of time number Tn
=TIME(Hr,Ms,Ss)	Returns the time number of Hr,Ms,Ss
=YEAR(Dn)	Returns the year number of date number Dn.

Special Functions:

Special functions perform a variety of advanced tasks, such as looking up a value in a table, or providing other information. The various functions and their meaning are as follows:

Function	*Description*
=CHOOSE(X,V0,...,Vn)	Returns the Xth value in the list V0,...,Vn
=COLS(Rg)	Returns the number of columns in the range Rg
=ERR( )	Returns the value of ERR
=HLOOKUP(X,Rg,Rn)	Performs a horizontal table look-up by comparing the value X to each cell in the top row, or index row, in range Rg, then moves down the column in which a match is found by the specified row number Rn
=INDEX(Rg,Cn,Rw)	Returns the value of the cell in range at the intersection of column Cn and row Rw
=ISERR(X)	Returns 1 (TRUE) if X contains ERR, else returns 0 (FALSE)
=ISNA(X)	Returns 1 (TRUE) if X contains N/A, else returns 0 (FALSE)
=NA( )	Returns the numeric value of N/A
=ROWS(Rg)	Returns the number of rows in range Rg
=VLOOKUP(X,Rg,Cn)	Performs a vertical table look-up by comparing the value X to each cell in the first column, or index column, in range Rg, then moves across the row in which a match is found by the specified column number Cn.

INDEX

170

COMPANION DISCS TO BOOKS

COMPANION DISCS are available for most books written by the same author(s) and published by BERNARD BABANI (publishing) LTD, as listed at the front of this book (except for those marked with an asterisk). These books contain many pages of file/program listings. There is no reason why you should spend hours typing them into your computer, unless you wish to do so, or need the practice.

COMPANION DISCS come in 3½" format with all example listings.

ORDERING INSTRUCTIONS

To obtain your copy of a companion disc, fill in the order form below or a copy of it, enclose a cheque (payable to **P.R.M. Oliver**) or a postal order, and send it to the address below. Make sure you fill in your name and address and specify the book number and title in your order.

Book No.	Book Name	Unit Price	Total Price
BP		£3.50	
BP		£3.50	
BP		£3.50	
Name		Sub-total	£............
Address:		P & P (@ 45p/disc)	£............
		Total Due	£............

Send to: P.R.M. Oliver, CSM, Pool, Redruth, Cornwall, TR15 3SE

PLEASE NOTE

The author(s) are fully responsible for providing this Companion Disc service. The publishers of this book accept no responsibility for the supply, quality, or magnetic contents of the disc, or in respect of any damage, or injury that might be suffered or caused by its use.